D0493809

Please return or renew this item by the last date shown.

Libraries Line and Renewals: **020 7361 3010**

Web Renewals: www.rbkc.gov.uk/renewyourbooks

KENSINGTON AND CHELSEA LIBRARY SERVICE

STORMING THE FALKLANDS

MY WAR AND AFTER

TONY BANKS

ABACUS

First published in Great Britain in 2012 by Little, Brown
This paperback edition published in 2013 by Abacus

Copyright © Tony Banks 2012

The moral right of the author has been asserted.

A CIP catalogue record for this book
is available from the British Library.

ISBN 978-0-349-00019-0

Typeset in Bembo by M Rules
Printed and bound in Great Britain by
Clays Ltd, St Ives plc

Papers used by Abacus are from well-managed forests
and other responsible sources.

MIX
Paper from
responsible sources
FSC® C104740

Abacus
An imprint of
Little, Brown Book Group
100 Victoria Embankment
London EC4Y 0DY

An Hachette UK Company
www.hachette.co.uk

www.littlebrown.co.uk

In memory of my father and my brothers
Ernest and Roderick. And in memory of all service
personnel who have given their lives for their country and
for those who have suffered the effects of Post Traumatic
Stress Disorder (PTSD) – Combat Stress

CONTENTS

STORMING
THE
FALKLANDS

INTRODUCTION

The Falklands War was short, sharp and very, very nasty. It was not just Britain's last roll of the imperial dice – when we sent a task force of all three services eight thousand miles to reclaim a far-flung colony. It was also the last conflict in which Britain fought set-piece land battles, bombarded the enemy with artillery barrages and employed infantry charges. It was not a police action or a peacekeeping mission. It was all-out war in which two national armies tried to pound each other into submission by killing as many of the enemy as possible.

The fighting I experienced as a young soldier in the Parachute Regiment was terrifying and murderous. We fought at close quarters, clearing trenches of Argentinian troops with bayonets and grenades. At times, it was like something out of the First World War. I saw close friends killed and mutilated, crying for their mothers as the life ebbed from them. I witnessed terrible sights of wounded and badly burned men writhing, screaming in agony, and dying. But I was a para – a tough guy in one of the toughest outfits in the British Army – and all that death and destruction did not bother me. Or so I thought.

The bean counters say that the Falklands War cost the lives of 907 people, with 1843 others wounded. For many years, I believed those statistics. Now I know better. The invisible wounded – the men who came back with shocking experiences and moments of terror seared into their minds – have never been accurately counted. For them, the war never ended.

For years, I did not consider myself as one of them. Before the war, I was young, carefree and happy-go-lucky, always at the centre of a crowd. But after the Falklands, I would spend long nights alone, with only a bottle of wine or whisky for company, drinking myself into a haze to evade disturbing memories and nightmares. I became angry, moody and difficult, and my marriage disintegrated as a result. But I was relatively lucky: I managed to blot out the past and build a successful business, rather than slip down the slope of alcoholism, drugs and crime, as many of my old army pals did.

The success of my business led to an invite from Channel 4 to take part in its *Secret Millionaire* programme. It turned out to be one of the most rewarding things I have ever done. Witnessing the struggles of many fine people who were trying to improve the lives of some of Britain's poorest citizens in the Anfield area of Liverpool was both inspiring and humbling. But meeting one volunteer, Lee Sanger – a veteran from the war in Iraq who was suffering from post-traumatic stress disorder – put me in touch with feelings that I had suppressed for over two decades. I was launched on a journey of discovery that would introduce me not only to some of Britain's forgotten casualties but to my former foes in Argentina and eventually take me back to the Falkland Islands themselves.

I was appalled to learn that over three hundred British and five hundred Argentinian veterans – men whose minds and emotions had been mangled during the war – had taken their own lives over the past thirty years. In other words, almost as many ex-combatants have committed suicide as died in the land fighting itself. And that truly shocking statistic does not even include those veterans who died slow, lonely deaths from drink, drugs or poverty in run-down flats, gutters or police cells.

Through *Secret Millionaire*, I became involved with Combat Stress, a charity founded after the First World War to aid victims of shell-shock whom the government wanted to lock away in mental asylums. Thankfully, we have come a long way since then, but we need to do so much more. I was surprised to learn that, on average, PTSD does not develop into a full-blown illness until fourteen years after the events that caused it. So, in the years to come, a great many veterans from the wars in Iraq and Afghanistan will probably need our help, and we should be prepared to offer it. I can only hope that this book will help to raise awareness of – and support for – the essential work currently being undertaken by Combat Stress.

This is the story of my war, and of the British and Argentinian veterans who shared their experiences with me. It is also the story of how I found peace by tracking down an ex-Argentinian soldier by the name of Omar Tabarez and returning a war trophy – his regimental trumpet – which I had taken from him as he had boarded a POW boat in Port Stanley. He gave me a warm welcome and introduced me to his former comrades. Their generosity helped me to see them in a new light – as fellow, equally vulnerable human beings.

My war experiences and trip to Argentina confirmed my long-held belief that war is stupid, futile and the ultimate failure of politics. But then my return to the Falklands – where I visited the graves of fallen comrades and the scenes of so much suffering – made me question whether the war had been justified after all. The answer, when it came, surprised me.

I had gone to the Falklands as a proud member of 2 Para, and we had fought for each other. I was not a fan of Margaret

Thatcher or her brand of English nationalism, and I was cynical about the war even before I boarded the ship in Portsmouth. Yet, when I visited the Falklands, met the islanders and heard their stories, I felt a surge of pride in what we had achieved. I started to think that this might well have been Britain's last honourable war – a justified fight to defend our territorial integrity. Or maybe it is just that all wars are personal, and the Falklands War was *my* war.

Whatever the reason, I no longer felt ashamed to call myself a Falklands veteran. I could now see the conflict for what it was – a good job, well done. And I would do it all over again.

CHAPTER 1

I WANNABE . . . A PUNK ROCKER

Why are British railway stations always such stinking dumps?
I wondered as I gazed up at the cavernous canopy of rusting
Victorian steelwork and dirty glass that enclosed King's Cross
Station – the dreary terminus for the East Coast Line, the
umbilical cord linking London and Edinburgh.

I was eager to get home and meet up with my mates. My
Easter leave would be spent chasing girls, boozing on a heroic
scale and catching up with my family. But first I had to get
there, and the lengthy journey of nine hours or more up to
Dundee was a killer. I wearily joined the lengthening queue
that had formed in front of the ticket barrier and surveyed my
fellow travellers. They were the usual suspects: businessmen

booked on to the sleepers; well-dressed elderly Scots returning home from visiting prosperous sons and daughters in the
Smoke; a smattering of roughnecks with their carry-outs of
vodka and strong lager determined to get as much bevvy as
possible down their necks before they left Aberdeen for two
weeks on an alcohol-free North Sea oil rig. There were one
or two cabbage-heads, too: Royal Marines – our bitter rivals –
heading up to Condor, their base near the fishing town of
Arbroath on the Scottish East Coast. I could tell them by their
kit-bags and developed upper bodies from all the rope work
they did in training. Then I spotted some posh students –
blue-eyed and blond-haired Hooray Henrys. If it wasn't for
their tweed jackets, they could have been Hitler Youth. No
doubt they were stalwarts of St Andrews University's Officers'
Training Corps – just the sort of bright and shiny tossers who
ended up telling us Toms what to do.

My heart sank as the queue shuffled slowly forwards. It
would be a long night and I would have to find a seat away
from the roughnecks who smoked and drank like there was no
tomorrow. They would spend at least three hours loudly
boasting about the big money they earned in the North Sea
before the drink took hold and the singing started. The queue
seemed to take for ever. I thought, Why do these jobsworths
in British Rail think it's such a privilege for us to be served by
them and pay through the nose to ride in their crappy trains?

There was a blackboard ahead: 'Oh no, please God, not more "Delays due to engineering works."' But as we got closer, I made out the message chalked in six-inch-high letters: 'Attention. 3 Para. Return to Barracks Immediately.' It brought me up with a jolt. We had a tribal rivalry with 3 Para, and I was desperate to know why they had been called back to Aldershot, our base in Hampshire, and whether it would impact on us, too.

It must be something big, I thought as I headed off to buy a newspaper. The possibilities raced through my mind. Maybe more inner-city riots? The plods had struggled to cope in Brixton and Toxteth, and there was talk of us being called in. The Russians were bogged down in Afghanistan after invading three years earlier, in 1979, but surely we wouldn't get involved there. After all, it had twice been a graveyard for the British Army. Then my stomach churned. Maybe the IRA had launched a massive offensive in retaliation for the deaths of the hunger strikers the previous year? They were well tooled up and bitterly determined. I had been lucky not to be sent to Northern Ireland, where the paras were viewed as enemy number-one by the Republicans. They had already extracted a terrible revenge on us for the events of Bloody Sunday in January 1972, when fourteen civilians died after 1 Para opened fire on protesters in the Bogside area of Londonderry.

With my guts rumbling, I briskly walked through the acrid cloud of smoke and urine-stench that hung in the air of the station's entrance to buy a paper. I wasn't one of Maggie Thatcher's boot boys. I didn't fancy having a go at my own people. And I felt the same about Northern Ireland. I was a Catholic and knew the history of Ireland – all about the famine and the struggle for civil rights. I would do my job, though. I had taken the Queen's shilling and above all I was loyal to my mates in 2 Para.

There was no shortage of real or imagined enemies for British paratroopers in 1982. But when I bought a newspaper at the kiosk outside the station I was stunned. 'Fucksake!' I said to myself. It seemed that Scotland had been invaded. By *Argentina*!

I struggled to take it in. The only connection we had with Argentina was our dismal performance at the World Cup in 1978. Some members of the dedicated Tartan Army of Scotland fans were said to be still heading home, four years later. The Scottish team had been woeful, but I couldn't believe they'd provoked an international incident. Then, as I read on, it all became clearer. The 'Falkland Islands' in the headline were not, as I had initially thought, part of the Outer Hebrides. Instead, they were eight thousand miles away in the South Atlantic. They had long been coveted by Argentina, and now General Leopoldo Galtieri – that country's detested and dictatorial ruler – had tried to boost his popularity by seizing them. Our garrison on the islands was composed of Royal Marines, and the useless fucking cabbage-heads had been overpowered and captured by the invaders.

I rejoined the queue and managed to find a seat in the packed train. It was a smoking compartment and within minutes my eyes were stinging. Surely being designated a smoking compartment didn't mean that everybody *had* to smoke? Bugger it! I fished a few tins of Carling Black Label out of my kit-bag, stowed it overhead and settled into the corner next to a window. At least I had managed to dodge the rough-necks. Those guys thought they were tough, but they wouldn't have lasted two minutes with the Maroon Machine that was 2 Para.

As we finally left the station and headed north, I thought less and less of fighting Argentina. It would never happen. This was the end of the twentieth century, for Christ's sake. The politicians would sort it out. It was all bluster – wind and piss for show. As we rattled on, the beer was going down a treat. It was warm but wet and a wee taster of the mega amount I would soon be quaffing when I teamed up with my mates at home. After a few tins I dozed off and slept soundly for hours, only waking as the train shuddered into Leuchars. The tiny Fife village was home to an RAF fighter base – a front-line defence against the Russians. It was also the stop for

11

St Andrews, four or five miles away. Sure enough, the Hooray Henrys alighted, but my eyes were drawn to the military houses just across the road from the station. They were behind a high fence topped with rolls of barbed wire, designed to deter Irish bombers more than Russian ones.

I had vivid memories of those houses. I had spent my early childhood in one of them when my dad had served with the RAF, working with logistics and keeping the supplies running smoothly. I smiled when I thought of my older brother Roddy chucking me down the stairs and Mum giving him a walloping. I always seemed to smile when I thought of Roddy.

I wondered what mad escapade he would have in store for us this time. Roddy and I were very close. When we were small, if my sister Terry or I ever got in trouble, he would shout 'Hit me!' and jump in front of Mum to shield us. Mum once hit him with a broom handle and was then horrified to find out that he hadn't committed the crime she thought he had. But he replied breezily, 'Don't worry, Mum. That's one in the bank for the next time.'

Roddy didn't want to go on to further education, even though he was quite bright. He was more artistic than academic, and he got a signwriting apprenticeship. My home leave in Dundee was always full of adventure. Roddy would pick me up and come out with something outlandish like:

'Let's go scuba diving.' He always had these hare-brained schemes.

I asked, 'Have you done a diving course, then?'

'No, but I bought a book.'

And that was us off to Kingoodie, a deep-water quarry outside Dundee, from where they had hewn the stone for the Bell Rock lighthouse. Roddy had bought the kit from a newspaper ad and studied the book. His expertise was not in doubt . . . as far as he was concerned.

Another time, he came round and announced, 'Let's go paragliding!'

'Done a course?'

'No, but I've bought a book.'

So me and my mates from the Territorial Army – Gary Whyte, Stewart Hutchison, Kenny Bambury and Rab Henry – who were as mad as I was and loved getting involved in Roddy's crazy schemes – piled into his old Ford Sierra and headed for a disused Second World War airfield at Errol, near Perth.

En route, Roddy explained his technique. We would tie a rope to the car's tow-bar, two guys would hold the parachute open, a 'spotter' would stand up in the car, poking his head through the sunroof, Roddy would drive until the parachute took to the air, and that would be us – up, up and away. The protective clothing was an old boiler suit. What could possibly go wrong?

Kenny, a hardy landscape gardener from Dundee, was the first one to give it a go. He tripped and fell and got dragged along the runway. The skin was ripped from his shoulders and sides. It was a horrible sight. But he got up and said, 'Fuck it. It'll work.' So he tried again, and it *did* work. Smiles all round. When the next guy had a go the rope snapped and he landed badly, sustaining a broken arm and wrist. It was bloody scary but great fun.

Roddy was as daft as a brush. He was good-looking, with long light brown hair and a fashionable moustache, and while he was short, like the rest of us, he didn't have the family propensity to put on weight. He was left-handed, partial to the odd smoke of dope and could turn his hand to anything: he could play guitar and taught himself hypnotism after seeing an advert in the *News of the World* which proclaimed, 'Become a Hypnotist!' He sent away for the books and taught himself all the tricks. He got so good that he was soon doing shows under the stage name Ricky Arcari. He looked like the real deal, with a smart dinner suit, gold watch and chain, and patent-leather shoes. He was a real character. It would be great to catch up.

With a sudden jolt, the train started moving again and picked up speed for a few miles before we slowed down to trundle across the mighty bridge that spans Scotland's longest river, the Tay. This was the bit of the journey I liked best –

nearly home. To the west, the river disappeared into a rugged landscape of mist-covered mountains. To the east, the Tay flowed into the North Sea, with Broughty Ferry Castle guarding the sparkling estuary from the north shore and Tentsmuir Forest fringing the Fife coast to the south. It was a stunning and dramatic vista, but the sight that most warmed my heart lay straight ahead. Huddled on the northern shore of the river, Dundee tumbled down to the sea in the lee of the Law, a volcanic hill that dominated the city and hosted a huge war memorial to the four thousand Dundonians who had died in the First World War. This was my stamping ground. East, west, home is best, I thought, and excitedly pulled down my kit-bag before we were barely off the bridge.

I couldn't wait to sample Dundee's delights. I had missed local delicacies like Wallace's Scotch pies, onion bridies that dripped aorta-clogging grease and white pudding suppers, not to mention the foaming nectar that was McEwen's 80 Shilling. Then there were the carnal pleasures of Teazer's nightclub, with the possibility of a knee trembler in a city centre alley after the disco-goers had emptied out on to the pavement in front of the Auld Steeple. This holy site, where Cromwell's forces had once massacred the Scottish defenders, should have been sacred, but on a Saturday night the taxi rank would erupt in punch-ups and we would usually be in the thick of them.

Scotland had not always been home, as Dad had frequently been stationed elsewhere. But he and Mum had always tried to come back to have their kids. Dad insisted on that – just in case one of us turned out to be good enough to play football for Scotland. Talk about optimistic! In those days, you had to be born in the country you wanted to play for – not just have a Scottish granny, like some of our rugby and football players today. But Mum was too ill to travel when she was pregnant with me, so I was born in Aylesbury, close to Dad's base at RAF Medmenham. That was always annoying for me. I resented being teased and called a 'plastic Jock', so I tried to hide my birthplace.

We moved to an RAF base in Cyprus when I was just a baby. The family photographs show me with blond hair and tanned skin, wearing shorts and running around on idyllic sandy beaches – like one long holiday. But it wasn't like that for Mum and Dad. Cyprus was a hotspot in the 1960s, with the Greeks and Turks launching terrorist attacks against each other and ultimately the Greek Eoka-B Gang declaring all-out war on the British. It was a tense time. Six months after we arrived in 1962, terrorists threatened to bomb us, and the Americans decided to evacuate their families. It was terrifying for Mum and Dad, but great for us kids.

Dad was always a hard worker and was totally dedicated to his family. He was born in 1926 and left school just fourteen years later to work as a coal man. The authorities mistakenly thought he was a miner, and therefore exempt from national service, and it was 1951 before they realised their error and called him up. By then he had married Mum, and my oldest brother, Ernest, was already two years old. Dad went into the RAF and after his two compulsory years were up he decided to stay on. It was a good career move and he got on quickly. He was like an accountant, monitoring stock and stores. The new job meant a lot of travelling and the family was stationed all over England as well as Germany and Cyprus.

Dad was short, with light brown hair and greying sideburns, and was always well dressed and smart. He was a clever man and very straightforward, always calling a spade a spade. As a boy, he had been offered the chance to go to grammar school, but instead he chose to stay with his mates and go to St John's, a junior secondary school. That decision was a bugbear for the rest of his life, because he realised he could have made more of himself than he did. As a result, he always pushed us hard to get a decent education.

Mum and Dad were both Dundonians, born and bred. My grandparents had all worked in the textile mills that earned the city the title 'Juteopolis'. The jute industry ruled Dundee's economy, with the giant mills churning out thousands of square miles of sacking and carpet backing each year. Mum was born in 1930 and left school at fourteen to work in the mill, where she learned the 'Mill Talk' sign language that the weavers and spinners used to communicate above the deafening clackety-clack of the looms. They would stroke their chins to warn each other that a gaffer or foreman was coming and pat the air above their heads to indicate a top hat – meaning that a manager was on his way. It was poorly paid, hard and dangerous work. The mills were incredibly noisy, filled with jute fibres and dust, and the workers could easily lose fingers, or even whole hands.

Even though I'm Scottish through and through, Banks is an English name, and Dad's family originally came from the fishing port of Grimsby. They were fisherfolk who moved up to Aberdeen for work and then gradually came down the coast until they ended up in Dundee. Dad was from a Catholic family of seventeen and Mum from a Protestant family of thirteen. Mum attended one of the few mixed schools in Scotland: St Michael's. The sectarian divide was never as big an issue in the east of Scotland as it was in the west, but the pupils still had different playtimes and were kept quite separate, on either side of the school site. When she came to marry Dad, Mum had to convert to Catholicism, but it was never a big deal to her.

By the time we went abroad with the RAF, my oldest brother Ernest was attending Lawside Academy, Dundee's

Catholic grammar school. He was obviously university material and it was decided that he should stay with my grandfather to avoid disrupting his schooling.

We returned to Dundee when Dad was discharged from the RAF, but before long he and Mum decided to emigrate to Canada – something they had planned to do before he was called up. So we upped sticks and headed for Hamilton, Ontario, where Mum's sister Betty had been living for several years. Once again, we left poor Ernie behind. He went to Aberdeen University to study law, which meant that he never really grew up with the rest of the family and that I never got to know him properly. I think that being left behind affected him deeply, and he had a bit of a chip on his shoulder because of it. He was also different from the rest of us: for instance, he was very devout, attending mass every Sunday, which none of the rest of the family bothered to do.

I was six years old when we emigrated, my sister Terry was eight and Roddy was thirteen. It was quite a culture shock for all of us. There were so many differences. I didn't have to wear a uniform to school – just jeans and a casual shirt. They didn't play football either, but I enjoyed trying baseball and basketball. Ten-pin bowling was another big thing, and we would all go along as a family.

At first, we lived with Auntie Betty, and one night I casually picked up the newspaper to check what was on television.

Betty was amazed because her eldest kid, who was two years older than me, couldn't read yet. In Canada, they didn't start school until much later, and the Scottish system was really good in those days, so I was way ahead of kids my own age. Within a fortnight, the school had put me up two age groups.

Hamilton was an industrial city, a steel town where every second person seemed to be Scottish, so it didn't take Dad long to find a job. Our first house was in a new development in an area that was always referred to as 'up the mountain'. It was a new, spacious terraced home surrounded with green grass and open spaces for us kids to play in – such a contrast to Dundee, where we'd had to make do with a patch of derelict land behind a tenement. We got into the Canadian culture of wearing jeans, baseball caps and T-shirts. We went to barbecues, which were a real novelty, and to drive-in movies. It was great.

But then disaster struck. Dad fell ill and needed a big heart operation. The RAF paid for it – he had a good pension from them – but Mum didn't feel financially secure over in Canada. So we returned to Scotland with nothing, not a pot to piss in.

We stayed with my grandfather when we first got back, before securing a lease on a house in the Hilltown. This was an area of crumbling tenements that had been hastily constructed for the country folk from Ireland and Scotland who had swarmed into inner-city Dundee in the nineteenth century to work in the mills. It says a lot about the rural poverty of the time that overcrowded, grimy Dundee was considered preferable. Our house, number three, was at the foot of the hill – a Victorian slum with the close entrance sandwiched between two of the roughest pubs in a rough old town. The Hawthorn Bar was on one side and the Central Bar on the other. At night, men would spill out of the pubs, pissed, singing, shouting and swearing. Some of the Hilltown boozers still had sawdust on the floor. Women were not allowed in the public bars, but a few of the lounges had little notices on the doors announcing that they were for 'Ladies and Couples Only'.

Even though the pubs were tough and raucous, they were mysterious and alluring – bright, warm beacons in a cold, monochrome landscape. A big part of their attraction was that they offered men an escape from squalid, overcrowded housing. Dad liked a drink but only on Friday nights, and only if he could afford it. It must have been great for him to get out of our flat, which had newspapers stuck on the windows instead of curtains. There was an outside toilet, which we shared with several other families, and no bath. Five beds were lined up in a row in the living room because that was the only room we could heat with the coal fire. The whole place was rickety and the floors were on a slant: if you put a penny in the middle of the living room, it would roll into the corner. There was a year-round smell of damp wood and decay. For some reason, we had a doll's table, which was where we ate our dinner. We didn't have a single matching cup or plate in the house. Everything had been given to us and cobbled together. We'd had to sell everything we had in Canada just to pay for our tickets home.

But as a child I never felt that we were poor or went without. If you didn't eat your tea, that was it, you went hungry, because there was nothing else. Grub was nothing fancy: fish fingers, chips and peas, mince and tatties, stew, soup. I never got much in the way of pocket money, but Dad used to play games with me, putting both hands behind his back and asking me to pick which one contained a penny. If I got it right, I got to keep the penny.

But then things started to pick up. Dad got a job as a storeman at Lowden's, an electrical supplier, and Mum opened a fruit shop in the Wellgate. It was quite a brave, entrepreneurial thing to do, but she knew what she was doing, having worked for a greengrocer when she was a young girl. I used to love going down to the shop, which was in a warren of buildings just across the road from our house and down some steep steps.

When Dad started working, his first purchase was a big zinc bath from the ironmonger. We would fill it with buckets of hot water, boiled on the hob, and my sister and I would bathe together. It was a step up in the world. Before then, I had to go with Dad to the public baths in order to get a wash. You would pay for your allowance of hot water, but you never controlled the tap: that was the attendant's job. If the hot water ran out, you just had to grin and bear the freezing cold or get out.

I had to do my chores first thing every morning: it was my job to set the fire and go downstairs to the baker's for the bread rolls. One morning, as I was kneeling next to the fire, I heard a sudden thump from one of the tenements opposite. I looked out the window and instantly recoiled, shocked to see the body of one of our neighbours splattered all over the pavement. He had committed suicide by jumping out the window. It was my first sight of a dead body. It would not be my last.

After breakfast, I would catch a double-decker to St Vincent's Catholic primary school, on Linlathen Road. (Legend had it that Dundee Corporation painted all of its buses green because they only employed Catholics!) I always liked school, and I was in the top group, but at that time I was only really interested in football. I'd get to school early and play until the bell rang for class to start. During breaks, we would occasionally re-enact the Second World War and play Japs and British, just to break up the day, but it was mainly football for us. After school, we would play some more, usually on a bit of wasteland behind the tenements. All the local kids gathered there and kicked about among the rubble. That was our main pastime. We didn't have many toys, and certainly no bikes, just a ball. Evenings were spent inside with my sister Terry. We would read, do our homework and make toast on the coal fire.

Our one big treat came on Saturday mornings, when we bombed down to the Gaumont Cinema for the 'Saturday Club'. All the mothers dumped their kids there and then went shopping. The older kids upstairs would flick peanuts or slowly drip ice-cream or tomato sauce from their hot dogs down on to the necks of their victims below. The attendants – in maroon jackets and peaked caps – would move among us, threatening to chuck out the miscreants. Then the lights were dimmed and the film, usually made by the Children's Film Foundation, would start in glorious Technicolor. The baddies were booed, the goodies were cheered, and we sang along to the tunes. It was such a contrast to tenement life.

My mum's brother Alex had a scrapyard in Rosebank Street, further up the Hilltown. His house was always full of kids, loads of them, some of whom I didn't even know. I always thought it was a dirty place, especially compared to our flat, which was spotless. Mum and Dad were very house proud and would send us kids off to mass every week so they could clean up. By contrast, my uncle was a typical scrappie – always filthy and dressed in an old oil-covered boiler suit – but I loved him, because he would give me a few bob for helping out at the scrapyard. I'm not sure I was much use, but it was good fun wandering about there, among all the old cars and piles of junk.

The yard entrance was squeezed between two tall buildings and had a forbidding front gate topped with coils of barbed wire. Inside there were two huge, snarling German shepherds that were chained up all day. I was terrified of them and never went near them. At night, my uncle would get me out the yard and then let the dogs loose. There was a caravan in the corner of the yard where the guys sat and had their cups of tea in oil-stained cups. Customers would come in and ask for a car part, and my uncle or his son would head off into the darkest recesses of the yard and always come back with the right thing. God knows how they did it. Nothing was catalogued or anything like that. And I don't think much money made its way to the taxman – they only dealt in cash.

Our uncle's example inspired Roddy in one of his earliest enterprises. The sixties and early seventies were an era of slum clearance in Dundee, with decay and dereliction all around us, so Roddy hit on a scheme to rip old pieces of lead and copper out of condemned buildings. We called the scrap metal 'peek' and flogged it to our uncle. I was selected to crawl under the floorboards and into the roof spaces because I was the smallest. I would wriggle into nooks and crannies, breathless and with my heart thumping, to tug at lead and copper pipes before emerging triumphantly holding my trophies aloft. There would be a chorus from Roddy and his mates of 'Well done, Anthony! Go and get some more!' Then I was off again. It was exciting and thrilling . . . and profitable. I always liked to be part of a team, even back then.

We would buy sweets, lemonade and comics with the proceeds of our 'recycling'. To the annoyance of the old mill wifies waiting to buy their snuff, we would bunch around the newsagent's 'penny tray' and take ages to spend our earnings. There were bright yellow 'bananas' at seven for a penny, 'sports' wine gums at the same price, penny dainties, lucky bags, peanut brittle and lucky tatties. And all that sugar was washed down with copious amounts of Pola Cola or fizzy-orange Fergusade as we settled down to follow our heroes in the *Beano*, the *Dandy*, *Victor* and *Hotspur* – all comics produced in Dundee, the city of 'jute, jam and journalism'. My tastes gradually matured from Dennis the Menace and Desperate Dan to characters like Alf Tupper – a working-class hero styled the 'tough of the track' who would polish off a fish supper before defeating his posh rivals in long-distance races – or the Wolf of Kabul, a British intelligence officer on the North-

West Frontier in Victorian times whose faithful servant would despatch rebellious tribesmen with his trusty cricket bat.

Then came 1968 and an event that changed my life. It had nothing to do with student rebellions or riots. I became a Celtic supporter. This was a momentous but largely random decision. My choice had nothing to do with them being an Irish and Catholic side. I simply saw that they were top of the league when I looked in the newspaper and thought, That'll do me. I've supported them ever since.

I got the bug big time and used to cry whenever they were beaten. I was like Statto and knew everything about the team. I'd get a Celtic annual for Christmas and would study the players until I knew everything off by heart. It was a great era. Some of the Lisbon Lions, who had triumphed in Europe in 1967, were still playing: great footballers like Jimmy 'Jinky' Johnstone, Bertie Auld and Tommy Gemmell. Then came Davie Hay, Kenny Dalglish and Lou Macari. I've been fortunate enough to see them all.

I'd take my transistor radio to bed with me and listen to Celtic playing European matches. The signal ebbed in and out, and the static meant I had to concentrate, but it was thrilling to hear the atmosphere and try to build a picture of the game in my head. I would wonder where Budapest Honved played, or where Luxembourg was, and enjoyed consulting the atlas to find out. The biggest game of all was probably the 1970 European Cup semi-final, when we beat Leeds in front of 136,000 people at Hampden Park. It was billed as the 'Battle of Britain', as 'Dirty, Dirty Leeds' were the big boys of the English game at the time. It was a great victory, but a few weeks later I endured the agony of watching us lose to Feyenoord in the final.

I collected bubblegum cards featuring the players and would swap them with my mates to get rid of the countless doublers, always searching for that elusive card that nobody seemed to be able to find. We would play games with them, flicking them off the wall and trying to land them on another card so we could win it.

I played in goal and would pretend I was the gangly Welshman who was Celtic's goalie, Evan Williams – even though I was about half his height. I was totally dedicated to Celtic and to football generally. I would go to any match, no matter who was playing, but I never paid. We would sneak in by scrambling under the turnstiles, or an adult would lift us over them. Nobody cared. Can you imagine being allowed to get away with that today?

But I could never understand the violence that seemed ever present at football matches in the sixties and seventies. On one occasion, I was watching Celtic beat Dundee at Dens Park with my dad when the Celtic fans started throwing bottles for no apparent reason. I thought, You're winning 8–1 and you're throwing bottles? I was too young to know that they were fuelled by drink. In those days, fans would take carry-outs into the ground. It was mad. Another time, we went to a Scottish Cup final, a midweek game at Hampden, and our bus was attacked by a sectarian mob armed with stones, bricks and bottles. It was terrifying for us youngsters, who didn't understand what it was all about. We just wanted to watch some football and these people were attacking us because of our supposed religion.

My first impression of the East End of Glasgow, around Celtic's ground, was that it was a terrible shit hole. The whole area was a slum, shocking even for a boy from Dundee's Hilltown! It opened my eyes to real poverty. But while it was rough and everything was run-down, I was thrilled to be going to Parkhead, the stadium where my heroes played. Mr Ferrie, our French teacher, drove us all down straight after school. It took for ever on the winding, slow road in the school mini bus. Then we were shepherded through the turnstiles, sticking together like glue. Groups of men were packed together as far as the eye could see, all singing the team songs. Then came the magical moment when we walked into the stadium and saw the hallowed turf. The floodlights were shining down and a fog of cigarette smoke was billowing above the bright green pitch. Everyone was smoking and drinking and singing and shouting. It was a crazy scene, but I was hooked and I've been going back ever since. Whenever I went to Parkhead or Hampden as a schoolboy, I used to wear cowboy boots as some protection from all the piss that flowed to the bottom of the terraces, where us kids usually stood. People would throw cans of urine into the crowd, too. It was barbaric, but I absolutely loved it.

I was also a passionate Scotland supporter, and Mum still has a letter I wrote to the *News of the World* in 1974, saying how great it was that we had qualified for the World Cup in West Germany. It was a star letter and the paper sent me ten pounds for it. For the first time in my life, I was rich! Four years later, I sat in front of the TV and watched Scotland lose 3–1 to Peru in the 1978 World Cup. That was the tournament we were supposed to win. We were 'On the March with Ally's Army'. Fifty thousand people had turned up at Hampden to see the team off to South America. Our manager, Ally MacLeod, was brilliant. He actually had the nation thinking we were going to win it.

Dundee's slum clearance had really gathered pace by the early seventies. The council had knocked down all the old slums and was in the process of building new ones – big estates on the periphery of the city, the type that Billy Connolly calls 'deserts with windows'. The ancient buildings in the Wellgate went first, and the Hilltown was next. We eventually moved to a three-bedroom council house in a new scheme on the western outskirts called Whitfield. We thought we had won the football pools! We were on the edge of farmland, so there were lots of fields to explore, and we even had plenty of proper football pitches. Terry got her own room, and the garden gave Dad a chance to potter. He always liked to keep busy and didn't watch much television. But he made a big exception for *The World at War*, narrated by Laurence Olivier, which we watched together religiously every week. Everybody we knew seemed to watch it, too. We would gather round our television set, us kids on the floor, hugging our scabby knees, and Mum and Dad on the couch, watching the unbelievable drama unfold. But during one episode Dad suddenly started crying and left the room, which was a shock for us, because he rarely showed his emotions. Newsreel of a ship exploding and sinking had just been shown. It was HMS *Barham*, a giant battleship that was sunk in the Mediterranean in 1941 with the loss of over eight hundred men. It was quite a while before I discovered that Dad's brother Archie had been one of the victims. It must have been terrible for him to see the footage of his own brother's death. Archie's medals are now among my most treasured possessions.

Dundee was surrounded by raspberry farms, and when our summer holidays – the 'seven weekies' – arrived, there was a mass exodus from the council estates to the fields. The braes of

Angus and Perthshire were Britain's great raspberry-growing belt, and between forty and sixty thousand casual pickers worked on the farms every year. For a lot of families, this seasonal work made all the difference, with the extra cash used to buy school shoes and uniforms. Over the summer, everyone seemed to have red-stained fingers and scratched hands from pulling berries – an unwelcome hazard of the job, especially for 'unemployed' pickers who had to sign on at the labour exchange in front of eagle-eyed clerks. It was a chance to make money but was great fun too, and the phrase 'It's the berries!' entered the Dundee vocabulary as an expression of total delight.

Filthy old buses and antiquated lorries would tour the housing schemes to pick us up first thing in the morning, and we would set off with our piece bags (an old gas-mask bag from the war was especially cool), each of which contained a picnic lunch of cheese sandwiches, crisps and a chocolate biscuit with juice or milk. Once we were in the fields, with the sun beating down on our necks and a prickly jute string tied around our waists, we would load punnets with raspberries for freezing or for sale as fresh fruit. If the berries were destined for pulp or jam, they were placed in a 'luggie' or bucket. We were paid threepence a pound, so some lads would bury stones in among the berries to increase the weight, hoping the farmer would not notice when the pails were emptied into barrels. But that was risky. If the stones were discovered among the berries, you were sent off the fields immediately. So we hit on a better way of increasing the weight: we started peeing on the berries! It worked a treat, but I have never felt quite the same about raspberry jam since.

Each picking season was great fun. It would not be long before berry fights would erupt, with us creeping up on our targets to pelt them with soft fruit. Sometimes we were rained off, but more often than not we went home sun-burned and happily weary, with money in our pockets, our piece bags stuffed with contraband berries, and our T-shirts splattered with the tell-tale red smudges of berry fights.

Me and my pals were always running around, keeping an eye out for any opportunity to earn a few extra pennies. But we got a bit carried away during one YMCA flag day. My pal discovered that if we peeled the stickers from the bottom of our cans, we could reward ourselves for our efforts. But he was caught when his dad asked him where all his pennies had come from. A sound belting was duly administered, and I was next in line when my mate's dad told my father what we had been up to. It was very rare for Dad to hit any of us (Mum was the disciplinarian of the family), but I got the hiding of my life. Even worse, I was put to work in the garden over the weekend and banned from going to the football. That was torture. In the distance, I could hear the roars from Dundee

United's home ground, Tannadice, where Celtic were playing. I thought Dad would relent, but he never did. It was a hard lesson, but one well learned.

Mum and Dad had come from nothing, but they were certainly ambitious for themselves and, above all, for us children. In those days, working-class people tended to be terrified of debt, but Ernie – now qualified as a lawyer – encouraged Mum and Dad to buy their own place and eventually they followed his advice. Our new home was in Nursery Road, Broughty Ferry, a former fishing village that had become a wealthy suburb of Dundee at the turn of the twentieth century. It was favoured by the jute barons who had made unimaginable fortunes in the textile trade. Massive mansions were concealed behind high walls, and it was said to be the wealthiest square mile in the British Empire at one time. However, as the jute trade died out, many of the mansions were subdivided and new houses were built in their gardens.

One of our neighbours was Jim Maclean, the manager of Dundee United, and Dad had even managed to buy a car. My parents felt that they had really arrived: a house in Broughty Ferry, a car and a son who was a lawyer! But Dad still worked as a storeman in a building company, and by now Mum was on the production line at Timex, the American corporation that had a huge watch-making factory in Dundee. Dad put his construction contacts to good use and wasted no time in building an extension. Dundee's building workers were firm believers in the redistribution of wealth, with men and materials routinely diverted from big civic and industrial projects to 'homers'. So it was no surprise that our extension bore more than a passing resemblance to the interior of the new Wellgate shopping mall.

I earned some pocket money by helping out the builders, but by now I had a regular job, too. Since the age of eleven, I had been getting up early to deliver the local newspaper before catching the seven-thirty bus to St Saviour's high school. The *Courier* was one of the last papers in Britain to appear with the front page covered in small classified adverts. It was produced by DC Thomson, the company which also published the *Dandy*, the *Beano*, *Topper*, *Victor* and *Hotspur* from an impressive red sandstone building in the city centre that was modelled on a Chicago office block. My paper round was great – a good carner – and I had the added perk of getting to read all the comics for free before I delivered them.

Ernie moved in with us in Broughty Ferry for a spell. At five feet three, he was even smaller than me. I towered over him by a full three inches! But then he and Roddy had a row with Mum and they moved out. (I sometimes wonder if the argument was about me, because both of my brothers used to complain that I got away with murder.) Ernie lasted only one night in their flat share, though. He was very much his own man, and couldn't put up with Roddy's disorganised way of life and general messiness. He came back to Nursery Road, but didn't stay long with us, either.

In the end, he opened the first new law practice in Dundee for generations. His business partner was another young local lawyer, Andy Lyall, a flamboyant character who dressed snappily – just as Ernie did – and always smoked a huge Havana cigar. They were among a wave of young working-class men who became lawyers in Dundee in the sixties and seventies. Many of them were Catholics too, with names like Donnelly, McGinley and Boyle. After school, I worked as a messenger for Ernie and Andy, delivering the mail and various missives, so I soon got to know all the solicitors' firms. It opened another world for me. All the office girls knew who I was, and there was plenty of banter. I was always told how important the job was, because these were *legal letters*, so I never dared go back to the office until they were all delivered. Some nights there would be a lot to hand over, which would piss me off, but other times there would be hardly anything and I would be done in ten minutes.

We were still going up in the world as a family. One Christmas I got a bike. Everyone else had a Raleigh Chopper, but I had a Dragster, which was much more cool, with a big gear stick in the middle and huge biker's handlebars. I thought I was the dog's bollocks.

Then came the chance of a school trip to Switzerland, and I was keen as mustard to go. I went home and told Mum that all my mates were going, but she said we couldn't afford it. I was devastated. But next day I came home from school and she suddenly said I could go after all. I suspect she was on the line at Timex and all the other mothers were saying how their wee Johnnies were going to Switzerland.

The trip to Switzerland was fantastic and not just for the *Sound of Music* scenery and an electrical storm that lit up the whole sky. It was a great adventure and a bit of a milestone for me. It started off with us nearly getting arrested in Belgium. All the kids had swarmed into the shop at a filling station like a plague of locusts and cleared the shelves – without paying. The owner called the police. They came on to the bus and we all looked pretty shamefaced as we emptied our pockets. We were later joined by a busload of older kids from Dingwall in the north of Scotland. I was fourteen at the time and they were older. They smoked, drank and shagged. It made a big impression on me. For the first time I also saw the teachers as human beings because they were smoking, drinking and shagging too!

Usually, my holidays were spent at RAF bases – like Colerne in Wiltshire or Kinloss in the north-east of Scotland –

so Dad could visit his old pals. We never went abroad. We would visit people we called 'Auntie and Uncle', and their kids were always older than me, so they would go off and play with Roddy and Terry, leaving me on my own. It wasn't all bad, though: in Colerne, my 'Auntie' Lily adored me, for some reason, and she would give me sweets and take me about. Her husband was a warrant officer, so he would take me to the ranges, which I thought was great. I spent whole summers with them, sometimes all seven weeks, because I'd get spoiled rotten down there. One year, the Concorde was being tested at Filton, near Bristol, and I saw it fly over Colerne. It had not been commissioned for service then, so that was a real thrill.

With Dad now a car-owner, there would also be Sunday excursions to Arbroath, Perth and other places like that. The car had a big bench seat in the front, so we'd have three up there and three in the back. I once managed to lock the keys in the car while we were in Perth, which caused a big drama. My uncle had to come all the way from Dundee to get us back into it.

I continued to like school, especially history and geography, which were always my two favourite subjects. But we were forced to choose between them at one point, so I had to ditch geography. PE was fun, too: I liked hockey and in the winter, when the football pitches were frozen over, we'd play footie with an ice-hockey puck. It was dangerous but fun.

My earning power was on the rise, too. I soon gave up my newspaper round to go up the next rung on the ladder. I went 'on the milk'. That meant more money and more freedom. The paper boys always looked up to the milk boys. They were older and cooler, and always battered the young ones when they passed by. I used to shit myself when I saw them in the morning on my paper round, and hid behind bushes to avoid them. Now I was one of them. *Yes!*

I started with Myles' Dairy in Long Lane, Broughty Ferry. I was the new boy on the lorry, but once I was accepted they treated me well. They were a good bunch of lads and they soon let me in on the tricks of the trade. Being up so early, at 5 a.m., it felt like you had the whole town to yourself, including the fresh baker's rolls that were delivered outside still-closed shops, which we would greedily snaffle. It was bloody freezing in the winter and I would wear loads of layers. I would even wear my granny's knickers to keep warm. But we would tear about the place and soon warm up. Before long I knew Broughty Ferry like the back of my hand. I knew the side streets, short cuts, where the good fruit trees were, the apples to pinch. And I used to drink about five pints of milk a day – another perk of the job.

I started even earlier on Saturday mornings, cleaning the

bottles and getting the lorries loaded up for deliveries. I was earning ten pounds a week, which was a lot of money for a young teenager, and that was without tips! I bought my own record player and every Saturday went down town to buy a new album. I was the envy of all my school pals, with the latest albums by Roxy Music, Bowie, Pink Floyd, Led Zeppelin, Bad Company and the Rolling Stones.

Our driver was an old English guy, Eric. He was a good bloke, but very slow and a bit grumpy. He never rushed. The round would take him as long as it would take him, and it drove us nuts. On Thursdays, though, Eric was off and one of the younger guys would drive. He wanted to finish early, so we flew about the streets, barely able to hang on. We'd have competitions, timing ourselves to see how quick we could do it.

In the school holidays, when the round finished about 7 a.m., I would stay on and go around with Eric for the day. I didn't get paid, but I enjoyed it and had bugger all else to do. I was soon top dog on the lorry and was hard on the youngsters, punching them in the mouth if they played up. There were two other dairies in Dundee – Kerr's and Fitchet's – and the rival crews of milk boys would clash whenever their paths crossed. When the lorries passed each other, we would be hanging off and swinging punches at one another. It was crazy stuff but pretty harmless, unlike the gang culture which prevailed in some of the housing schemes.

We delivered cream and eggs as well as pints of milk. We had milk bottle carriers, wire with plastic coating, and carried twelve bottles. An empty crate would be dumped at the end of the street for our empties, and the next full one would be ready for us, because the route was all planned out. We'd be sprinting, sweating our balls off, and really going for it. The quicker you got it done, the quicker you would be finished.

I can't even drink full milk now, but back then you couldn't really get semi-skimmed. The cream always sat on the top. There would be complaints to the dairy because birds would peck through the milk-bottle tops for the cream, so we would put plastic ice-cream containers on top to keep the sparrows away. And you had to put the milk in exactly the right place every day or customers would kick up a fuss.

I was making great money on the milk, but soon I hit on another earner when a pal helped me get a job after school. My official title was 'chicken catcher'. I'd get the bus out to Mitchell's of Letham, a big poultry breeder around twelve miles from Dundee, and go into these huge, dark chicken sheds, covered in dust and shit. Another boy would catch the chicken and hand it to me. I would grab it, take it to a window in the shed and pass it out to a guy who would load it into the lorry. Of course, the chickens didn't take this manhandling lying down. I'd get scratched and pecked and cut to pieces. When I got home, Mum would make me change out of my chicken-shit-covered clothes in the garage and I would bolt back into the house in just my underpants.

With two jobs, I was positively loaded, which was just as well because I had a very active social life and was about to develop a passion that would rival even Celtic – girls. As a little kid, I had been a wee ball of energy; now I was a testosterone-charged wee ball of energy. Along with two pals from the milk round, Ian and Don Strachan, I'd go to the YMCA discos at St Aidan's church in Broughty Ferry. The adults searched us on the way in, but we'd head straight to the toilet, and other guys would pass booze through the window and then come in themselves. That was when I first started drinking. Sometimes we'd down a quarter-bottle of vodka in the park before going inside. We got lifted by the police one night, for drinking cider, and I couldn't decide whether to tell my dad. In the end I did, and he made the right noises about being disappointed in me. He kept me inside for the weekend, which was torture for me, because I loved being outside. But I could tell that he knew it was inevitable I would start drinking one day, and nothing he did would make me stop now.

I had a real mix of friends in the Ferry – some from my school, St Saviour's in town, others from the Grove Academy, which was in the Ferry itself, posh kids from the fee-paying

Dundee High School, and others from all walks of life and religions. My first girlfriend was a doctor's daughter who attended the High School. She was very good-looking, and her parents always seemed to be out, so we were usually round at her place. For some reason, though, I dumped her and started going out with a lassie from a big council scheme. Mum was devastated. When I'd been with the doctor's daughter, she'd reckoned we were halfway to joining the aristocracy.

I liked girls, and for some reason they liked me, too. On one occasion, Mum and Dad put the house on the market, but they failed to tell me that people were coming round to view it. I was with my current girlfriend in my bedroom when the door suddenly burst open and in walked the estate agent with the prospective buyers. Talk about teenage angst! Another time, Mum came home early from work and I had to stuff my girlfriend in the wardrobe. She was in there for three hours before I was able to sneak her out the front door.

After Broughty Ferry, we moved to Arbroath Road. It was a wee cottage, a shell of a house, but they bought it so Dad could build his own house in the garden and not have any debt. Mum and Terry went to live with my auntie in Douglas, while Dad and I stayed in a caravan round the back of the cottage. It was basic stuff – no running water and every morning we chipped ice off the windows. My bed was like a ball of hamster bedding. The plan was to do up the cottage, move in there, then get planning permission and build another house where the caravan was standing. Eventually, Dad managed to do all that.

Around this time, though, I received a shattering blow. Having grown up in and around the RAF, my great ambition was to be a pilot. But during a school medical I was told I was colour blind, which ruled me out. That left me gutted and angry. I had done OK at school, getting five As and a B in my O levels, but I didn't pick enough subjects in my Highers to keep me busy, so I spent much of my time doing other things.

Four of the lads at school formed a punk rock band that belted out enthusiastic covers of Sex Pistols, Clash and Ramones songs. I thought they were just great and appointed myself their manager, roadie, everything. We organised the gigs together – at the school and in local halls, church halls and the YMCA. I made sure we got there safely, got the gear inside and sorted out tickets. We'd be lucky to make twenty quid a night, but it wasn't about the money. It was about thinking we were punk rockers.

On stage, the lads got more abuse than anything else. The crowd would spit at them and throw stuff, but it was punk rock after all, so that was part of the scene. Scott Gowans, our rhythm guitarist, reckoned he was quite cool, so he wore grey flannel trousers that were tapered in, Doc Martens and thin ties. But our singer and lead guitarist, a guy called Neil Mitchell, was much more out there. He would dress in ripped shirts and ripped jeans, not giving a fuck, but that was cool in another way because he was so grungy. We were the only punk band in our year, so those who were into that type of music would all come to the gigs and jump around, pogoing, crashing into each other.

The Sex Pistols and the Clash were all the rage, but we were also into the Undertones, Roxy Music, the Ramones, the Rolling Stones, the Who, Black Sabbath and Pink Floyd. We all listened to Radio 1 to hear the latest tunes – John Peel at night and Noel Edmonds in the morning. Bands on tour would play the Caird Hall in Dundee, and I usually managed to sneak in for free. When the bands came to town, I'd go down, hang out at the goods entrance and ask the roadies if they wanted a hand with the gear. After a bit of helping out they'd let me inside for nothing. Sometimes I still didn't manage to see the whole gig, though: at a Boomtown Rats concert, I was thrown out for jumping up on the stage and giving Bob Geldof a load of abuse.

Anyone who knew me back then wouldn't have been surprised, because I was starting to lose it. There was nothing to keep me interested and I started getting into trouble. I was eventually expelled for flushing a lassie's head down the toilet. It was near the end of term and Mum was called in to see the headmaster. I'd been in bother throughout the year, and he basically said to me, 'You know, you could leave school and go to Dundee College, and get paid money for that.'

That captured my attention. Get paid for going to school? Yes, please, I'll have some of that. I left school with four Highers – history, English, economics and modern studies. I failed my maths Higher twice, which was terrible, but the teacher was pretty poor. She was off ill all the time so I lost interest in the subject, and that was that.

Education was everything for my parents. They had worked hard and gone up in the world. Ernie was doing well as a lawyer, Roddy had a trade as a signwriter, and Terry was going to be a nurse. With my hopes of becoming a pilot shattered, Dad started to push me into accountancy. But by this time, I thought I was a big punk rocker. One night, I came down the stairs wearing Dad's old RAF shirt, with a rip across the chest and a safety pin for aesthetic purposes, a makeshift thin tie, an undertaker's cloak, a pair of grey flannels and a pair of Doc Martens up to my shins. Dad took one look at me and went apeshit: 'If you want to dress like that, you can get out of here.'

That was a shock to the system, but I wasn't prepared to back down, so I moved in with Roddy in his flat in Douglas. By now, he was divorced and living on his own, but he would occasionally go away to work on the trawlers. After one trip, he brought me back a whale's tooth. He was also well into his hypnotism, and my girlfriend was his first 'victim'. Living with him was fun for a while, but it didn't last. Roddy was a smoker and always had dope in the house. That wasn't the life for me. It didn't take me long to miss the comforts of home, and eventually I went back with my tail between my legs.

I was going to have to buckle down.

CHAPTER 2

THE MAROON MACHINE

My father loved the idea of having a lawyer and an accountant in the family. Like most people in those days, both he and Mum respected all the professions. Having returned home, I gave in and was duly enrolled for an accountancy degree at Dundee's Bell Street College of Technology, which is now Abertay University. But from day one, I knew I wasn't going to like the course. It suddenly dawned on me that I would be stuck as a bean counter for the rest of my life, and that just didn't do it for me. I tried to get on with it, but every day I went in, the fear grew stronger.

After a few weeks, I started looking for ways to earn some extra cash to supplement my grant of around five hundred pounds. That was a lot of money, and it arrived in a lump sum, but my love of alcohol meant it wasn't going to go far. One day I saw an advert in the local *Evening Telegraph* about parachuting, and I thought, That'll be exciting. I became even more interested when I noticed that they were offering money for it, too. After looking at the small print, I realised that it was an ad for the Territorial Army, and I decided to sign up.

I found myself sitting in the office of the TA drill hall on my eighteenth birthday. I had a broken thumb and my arm in a sling as souvenirs of a recent punch-up. By this time, my angry wee man syndrome had taken a real grip and I would challenge anyone if they so much as looked at me the wrong way. And I would never back down. My attitude was: 'You might beat the shit out of me, but I'm going to make sure your nose will be bust, or your nipple will be hanging off, or something.' The other guys in the waiting room were mean, hard-looking bastards, but I scowled and swaggered to look mean and hard, too.

I had no idea about military life until I joined the TA. Then, before long, I knew I wanted to join 2 Para. It was not a local regiment like the famous Black Watch, but I found out a lot about its colourful history, including the fact that it had begun life as a Scottish regiment. I discovered that the British paras had been set up at the behest of Winston Churchill after crack German paratroops had displayed airborne soldiers' potential during the Battle of Crete. Their first real test was a bit of a damp squib. Operation Colossus was supposed to hamper the Italian war effort by destroying a giant aqueduct near Calitri in southern Italy. The mission succeeded, but the aqueduct was of dubious importance and all of the paras were captured, including one group who were tortured and then murdered by Mussolini's Blackshirts. A lot of difficult lessons were learned, though, and the next effort was a triumph.

Operation Biting was a daring mission into France to steal specialised radio-tracking equipment. Known as the Bruneval Raid in the press, it took place in 1942. It was so amazingly audacious that it might have been dreamed up by a Hollywood scriptwriter. A force of 120 men from 2 Para, mainly drawn from Scottish regiments, including the Black Watch, the Cameron Highlanders, the Seaforth Highlanders and the King's Own Scottish Borderers, were dropped on a cliff-top near Le Havre, along with a radio expert – Flight Sergeant C. W. H. Cox. Their task was to steal the top-secret German Wurzburg apparatus with the aid of intelligence supplied by the French Resistance.

They took the Germans completely by surprise by dropping from Whitley bombers at just 600 feet before seizing the equipment and taking an operator prisoner. They then scrambled down to the beach below, where they escaped under a hail of German fire when the navy sailed in to save them with all guns blazing. 2 Para suffered just two casualties, with six others taken prisoner. As the flotilla made its way back to Portsmouth, the destroyers played 'Rule Britannia' over their loudspeakers.

You just couldn't make it up. This was definitely for me!

The success of the Bruneval Raid persuaded the War Office to expand the parachute force rapidly, and throughout the rest of the war they saw action in North Africa (where the Germans dubbed them 'the red devils'), Sicily, Italy, Normandy and finally, of course, Arnhem – where they fought heroically in defeat in the desperate and doomed 'bridge too far' battle.

During the Cold War, the paras' main function was to serve as an elite force that would spearhead our efforts to prevent the Soviet Red Army from advancing across the plains of Germany. But the regiment soon found itself acting as fire-fighters and 'peacekeepers' as Britain withdrew from its empire while simultaneously trying to suppress nationalist and communist rebellions. They saw action in nearly every colonial hotspot, from Suez and Cyprus to Aden and Malaya, but they were never intended to be a counter-insurrectionary force, so they were never coached in how to win 'hearts and minds'.

Instead, the paras were crack soldiers who were trained to take on other elite forces. They were steeped in aggression and taught how to kill and maim, disable, paralyse and eliminate.

At no time during my training was I coached in flower arranging or how to make a nice cup of tea. So using the paras as a police force was always bound to end in tears – as it did in Northern Ireland. The events of Bloody Sunday led to a series of Republican reprisals against the regiment, from the bombing of the Aldershot barracks just a month later to the Warrenpoint massacre in 1979. In all, fifty-one paras died during the Troubles.

As a Catholic, I knew about Northern Ireland and the civil rights issues. I was even a bit of a nationalist, and I didn't agree with what the British were doing there. But the Territorial Army quickly took hold of me and my life. And thank God it did, because the student life was definitely not for me. The college was in the centre of town, and I soon found that it was easier to go for a beer than attend classes. We used to drink at the local student pub, the Bread, right on the edge of the campus. I called it my office because I spent all day there. My pals knew they were likely to find me in there. My staple lunch came from the pub menu: a Scotch pie, a packet of crisps and a pint of lager.

I didn't much like my classmates, and I was still living at home, not in student halls. Wandering around town, I would meet a lot of guys from the TA, many of whom were unemployed, and they would invariably drag me to the pub. You built up quite close relationships in the TA, because, unlike the regular army, you all came from the same area. You went to the same schools, your families knew each other and you played football against each other. And we were all volunteers, of course.

What really got to me about college was the air of superiority that the would-be accountants had. They truly believed they were better than everyone else. I never understood that. I went to classes for most of the first term and occasionally in the second term, but when the third term came along I just collected my grant cheque. That was the end of college life for me, and I dropped out. Looking back, I occasionally think it's a travesty that I never got a degree, especially as everyone seems to have one now. I interview people who are supposedly 'educated' up to their eyeballs, but there is no way I would give them a job.

I learned far more in the TA than I ever did – or would have done – in college. And you had to learn fast, or you knew you would suffer. If you fucked up, you had to run up a hill or do press-ups on the icy ground. It was like training dogs: after a couple of smacks, a dog generally learns not to piss on the carpet. I liked the challenge, despite the pain. I was given brand-new boots for my first march. It was only six or eight miles, but the stiff leather gave me massive – and incredibly painful – blisters on my feet. It was a real struggle. My mate Dougie Craig dragged me around the course and helped me to the finish. 'Just go through it,' he said. 'Keep going. Go through this and everything will be easier. Break in your boots and they will be the comfiest things ever. Come on.' I made it to the end, collapsed and peeled off the boots. My socks were soaked in blood, the blisters were horrendous, and I was in agony, but I looked around and everyone else was in exactly the same boat, including Dougie. Suddenly, I felt elated and thought, Actually, I quite enjoyed that. Let's do it again.

Tuesday night was drill night. A four-ton army lorry with bench seats and a canvas roof would pick us up at Dundee train station and drive us across to St Andrews. Some guys occasionally chose to run the fourteen-odd miles instead. On weekends, we would be picked up at 5 p.m. on Friday night and driven over. We'd get our stuff ready, packing kit, in anticipation of getting up at 4 a.m. to go jumping at Leuchars or Edinburgh, where the giant Hercules aircraft would come in each Saturday. Then it was back to Dundee late on Sunday afternoon.

Our regular permanent staff instructor, Chris Williford, was brilliant. He got the numbers up at St Andrews to such an extent that he eventually commanded two platoons. We were all young and naive, and were enthralled by him. One day, he said, 'Right, lads. Tomorrow it will be helicopter training.' We were all excited at the prospect of training with a chopper. The next day, we went into the drill hall and saw that he had chalked out the floor plate of a heli-copter, complete with plastic seats for the pilots. That was the nearest we got to a real helicopter that weekend. But it worked. He taught us how to get in and out of a helicop-ter safely, what to avoid, how to pack our kit. He knew that in a few weeks we'd be on a big exercise in Germany and would be doing all this shit for real. We might have felt a bit daft jumping in and out of an imaginary helicopter, but it definitely helped.

We were totally self-contained in St Andrews, with our own drill hall and accommodation. We would go on training exercises, often down to the Sands beach, where they filmed the classic running scenes for *Chariots of Fire* – in which some of my mates appeared as extras. After training, we were free to roam the public houses of the 'home of golf' at night. And there was plenty of totty – much of it posh – in this student town. The girls always enjoyed spending some time with us army boys. I suppose we were a bit of rough for them. We'd go to the students' union and cause carnage, and we had the perfect chat-up line when last orders were being called at 11 p.m.: 'Do you fancy coming back to the barracks for another drink?' Our place was open until about 4 a.m. There were some big, big nights in there, with loads of drink and women all over the place. There was an unwritten rule that you could bring back as many girls as you liked, but you had to get them out of the building by morning. So there were some classic walks of shame when the sun was coming up.

If you were a good attender – which I and a lot of other guys from my platoon were – you definitely reaped the benefits. They knew you would always turn up, volunteer for everything and make yourself available, so they made sure you got preferential treatment. If there were any courses up for grabs, we good attenders always had first refusal. So I was often away on weekend exercises or courses. I thought it was great to get trips down to the likes of Brize Norton, in Oxfordshire, especially as the TA paid you for your trouble. It was a trip away, a world apart from Dundee. The adrenalin rush of jumping, and the prospect of seeing the world in the future, really appealed to me as a teenager.

I was in the TA for about eighteen months, during which time I did a lot of jumps. The parachute instructors at RAF Brize Norton were always requesting volunteers – lunatics who were prepared to jump out of planes or balloons on a static line at eight hundred feet – and I always stuck my hand up. The fly-boys and instructors were good value, and they seemed to have a great life: they didn't work weekends, they finished at 4.30 p.m., and they had two-hour lunch breaks. There were women on site, too, and the guys were on the piss every night. They had a nightclub which opened every Thursday night, and the food was phenomenal: they had steak bars, salmon bars, salad bars, anything you wanted. Going there was better than going on holiday. And we got paid for it! It certainly beat the hell out of sitting in accountancy classes.

I threw myself into army life. The guys I mixed with were from all walks of life – fellow students, guys on the dole, apprentice mechanics, labourers, dock workers, joiners, ex-convicts, everything. It really opened my eyes, because this disparate bunch of guys all came together to work as a team and support each other. Every weekend, we lived together, slept together, trained together and fought together. That generated real camaraderie. These days, most people go to university and get that *esprit de corps*, but I found it in the TA. I would go back to college and sit with my classmates, who felt they were superior to everybody else just because they had a few qualifications and were studying for a degree. But every weekend I escaped from all that and mixed with great guys from working-class backgrounds who looked after each other. It was the end of the seventies, and Britain was in a deep recession, but here I was doing great, exciting things. It made me reassess what I wanted from life. Coming back from Brize Norton, we'd go out on the tiles in London and end up sleeping in the toilets at Paddington Station because we'd spent all our money on grog. Gay guys would post notes under the cubicle door and we'd shout, 'Gays!' and chase them down the road, threatening them with all sorts of violence but never actually bashing them. It was all just great fun to us.

By then, Dad had taught me to drive in his old yellow Nissan Sunny 120Y. It was a four-speed manual and I loved it. Being mobile, going anywhere I wanted and driving the TA lads around opened up a whole new world for me. And it landed me a great perk when I got to drive a Land-Rover to Germany ahead of a major exercise in 1980. It was the biggest airborne exercise since the Second World War, with whole divisions taking part. I was still only eighteen, but I was one of the few guys who had a licence, and it was a huge adventure. We were part of the advance party and I drove our truck, with another guy, in a huge convoy from St Andrews to Hull, where we caught a North Sea ferry to Holland. Boarding the ferry, we met up with other TA regiments from all over the UK. The reception we got driving through Holland was unbelievable. The locals waved and cheered as we drove through towns that the British had liberated from the Nazis at the end of the war. I thought it was incredible that we were still seen as heroes some thirty-five years later, but I guess we never fully understood what it felt like to be liberated.

We arrived in Germany a week before the exercise was due to kick off. We helped set everything up, pitch tents, organise stores. It was a major operation, the Cold War was on and it was all taken very seriously. For the first time, I saw how the whole army worked together, alongside the RAF and Royal Navy, and now I knew for sure that I wanted to join the regular army. I loved the camaraderie, I hated college, and I yearned for something more exciting than being an accountant for the rest of my life. The thought of sitting in an office crunching numbers until I was sixty-five seemed a fate worse than death, especially once I'd been bitten by the parachuting bug.

I can vividly remember my first jump. It was at Brize Norton. We'd arrived on a Sunday, and the course started the following day. Your first jump would normally be out of a balloon on the Thursday, with Monday to Wednesday set aside for practice. We spent time on the fan, jumping from thirty feet up with the fan resistance slowing our descent to the ground, which allowed us to learn how to hit the ground in the correct fashion. All was going according to schedule, but then the weather was bad on the Thursday, so I was told my first jump would be out the side of a plane, not from a balloon. We were trucked to RAF Lyneham to be dropped on Weston-on-the-Green at Brize Norton. The plane was a C-130 Hercules. It was hot, sweaty and noisy, and we were in clean fatigues with no equipment, just our parachutes.

On your first jump, despite all the training, you have no

idea what is going on. Before you know it, you're out the back, there's turbulence, you're being thrown about, and then you feel the tug of the parachute. At that moment, all your training goes out the plane with you: your head is up your arse. But when you touch down, you're buzzing. That's it. Hooked for life. Let's do it again!

Strangely, though, the second jump is much more scary. In fact, it's the most scary jump you'll ever do. You know what's coming and you start thinking about it. I got through it, though, and after another jump out of the plane it was finally my turn for the balloon. Before I went up, a young guy my age came running past and I asked him how it was. He was a Dundee bloke called Norrie Elder who had lost his front teeth in a punch-up. He beamed a toothless smile and said, 'Better than shagging!' I was shitting myself as I watched guys stepping out of the balloon's basket into thin air, but when my turn came I had to agree with him.

From then on, I just couldn't get enough of it. You would be up early – at 3 or 4 a.m. – to get to the airfield when the weather conditions were at their best. Then you would lug your heavy gear on to the aircraft, haul yourself out of the plane, hit the deck and get yourself together. You would be tired and sore, and that was just the start of the day, because then you'd be off on an exercise. But the buzz and excitement never wore off. There was always adrenalin from the jumps and the low-level flying. I loved the smell of aviation fuel and still do to this day. It brings back a lot of good memories.

You had to do seven jumps to get your parachute wings, with some out of the plane, a few out of the balloon, one with full equipment, and one at night. I was as proud as anything when I got my wings. I was a fully fledged Tom – a private in the Parachute Regiment. But there was no way I could show them to my mates because the piss-taking would have been unbearable. And besides, everyone else was in the same position, so you just got on with it. But back in Dundee, I would go out on the town in my uniform. The girls loved it. It never failed!

Those seven jumps were the first of many. In the TA, we jumped more than the regulars because of our constant training and attendance at courses. I lost count quickly, but I reckon I clocked up about two hundred during my time in the Army. That is a lot of jumps. But the buzz, the surge of adrenalin, never diminished, even if it was the fourth or fifth jump of the day.

In the Parachute Regiment, the aircraft is the only means of transport. And while you train at eight hundred feet, in operations they drop you from four hundred feet. You don't need a reserve parachute because if your main 'chute doesn't open, you're dead. That's not the only danger, though. While the rules of war say that a pilot who ejects from a plane cannot be shot at, paratroops are considered legitimate targets. So the thing is to get out of the aircraft and down on the ground as soon as possible.

Coming from an urban environment, I'd never had the chance to shoot a gun, so I was excited by the prospect of getting my hands on one in the TA. But you never got near shooting a rifle or a machine gun until you could strip it down, clean it and put it back together . . . and you had to do all that blindfolded. We would race each other, time each other, to see who could do it the quickest. And you could never be parted from your rifle. In the regiment, you were expected to sleep with it. The same went for your Bergen rucksack. They taught you how to pack it right, so you knew where every single thing was. That way, when you were in the dark or under stress, you could go straight to whatever you were looking for.

These were all valuable lessons, and I was learning about other aspects of life, too. There were guys pissing their beds through too much drink, and changing their mattresses over before inspections. Some blokes had two mattresses – one to sleep on and one for inspections. I saw how men dealt with things – how older men dealt with eighteen-year-old boys. The continuous banter and dark, sick humour got people through tough situations. I remember being sent to the store before we went out on an exercise to pick up a sleeping bag.

I knocked on the door and the colour sergeant asked what I wanted. When I told him, he said, 'Well, what the fuck are you doing here? What does that sign say on the door?'

'"Store", Colour.'

'That's right. *Store*. It's for fucking storing things. If I was to issue things, it would be called the "issue store". Now, piss off.'

So off I went on the exercise, without a sleeping bag, thinking I was going to freeze my bollocks off. I was stressed out, shitting myself at the prospect of spending a night out in the hills with no protection from the cold, when one of the officers suddenly threw me one with a knowing smirk.

Once, at the wee bar they had in the TA barracks, I told my two mates that I'd get the first round of drinks in. I queued up diligently – there was certainly no pushing in – and when I was up, I asked for two pints of lager and a lager tops. The barman asked me bluntly to repeat my order, which I did. Then he told me to fuck off.

'What have I done?' I asked

'Lemonade in a man's drink? Fuck off.'

He made me go to the back of the queue and then served me three pints of lager, with no tops.

Six months later, sitting in the same bar, it was like *Groundhog Day* when I saw him pulling the same routine on the latest batch of recruits.

I loved this life and couldn't wait to do it for real. I wanted to prove myself.

My parents were appalled when I told them I'd decided to leave university. Ernie was doing well as a lawyer and was now dabbling in property, with Roddy doing up the flats for him. Terry was a qualified nurse. When I'd gone to college, my parents had thought I was sorted, too. But here I was, telling them I was dumping everything to go and get shot at.

While I was waiting to get into the regular army, I did a few bum jobs: I worked in a supermarket, then I emptied dustbins — not the plastic wheelie-bin jobs, but the big heavy drums that you hoisted on to your shoulder. They were always covered in crap, and cats' piss ran down your back, but it was good, honest work and I was happy to be mixing with honest, normal folk. I grew up very quickly in those few months.

A lot of my TA mates were in a similar position to me — doing whatever jobs they could find while they waited to join the army. We would meet up in the dingy basement bar of the Tay Centre Hotel, opposite the train station. Black Sabbath and Bad Company were the soundtrack to that particularly hazy part of my life. We would go out for a night and visit all four clubs in Dundee at the time — the Sands in Broughty Ferry, Teasers, Tiffany's and the Barracuda. There was a big crowd of us, often in our uniforms, and we were well known around town. Our ages ranged from eighteen to thirty-eight, and between us we knew all the bouncers, police and bar staff. Somebody always knew somebody.

One member of this group was Ally Melvin. He was from the Kirkton estate in Dundee and worked as a wood machinist, but he eventually got fed up, joined 2 Para soon after me, and ended up doing a full army career. But he narrowly missed the Falklands. Throughout training, I was in 472 Platoon and Ally was in 480, and he was just finishing when the conflict blew up. Another TA lad was Jimmy Falconer, who went into 3 Para.

Three or four of us would go out together and then meet up with the others. By the end of the night, there would be fourteen of us. You would go out with a tenner in your pocket, get pissed, have a fight, have a shag, have a Chinese and catch a taxi home. And you'd still have money left in the morning.

Whenever a fight broke out, it was all-in. I saw it happen so many times. We wouldn't always be standing with each other – some of us would be chatting up birds, or at the bar, or with other mates. But if one of us started scrapping, all the others would pile in immediately. We had one especially spectacular fight in Da Vinci's. Monday night was nurses' night, which was not to be missed. There was a bar on the first floor which overlooked the dance floor, and from up there you could see that the tiles on the floor were shaped into a phallic symbol that shot into jets at one end. Anyway, me and a mate were standing beside a portable gas fire when we got into an argument with two guys sitting beside us. Ten seconds later, it was all on, with fists flying. Next thing I knew, my mates had the two boys dangling by their ankles over the ledge above the dance floor. The barman vaulted the bar to try and stop this, but my pal Grant Whyte, who was no relation to my pal Gary Whyte, decked him, even though he was a mate of his. By now, some of the other guys were throwing whisky on the gas fire, sending flames leaping into the air. The two guys were eventually hauled back up and dragged out of the club, with their heads bouncing off the steps on the way down. They could've been killed, but at the time we didn't even think about it. I can't even remember what the argument was about in the first place. But this was Dundee in the late seventies. It could've been over anything.

One of my best mates around this time was Jim Purvie, known to everyone as the Swerve. He was a total character and could hold an audience in the palm of his hand with his stories and jokes. One day, me and big Grant Whyte – a bright spark who did civil engineering – were walking down the Seagate in town when we bumped into the Swerve.

He looked us up and down, grimaced at Grant – who we called Bucket-of-Shite, because no matter what he wore, he always looked like a bucket of shite – and said, 'Time for a pint, lads?'

Now, these were hard times for everyone in Dundee. Thatcher had just got in and unemployment was rising fast. I was one of the lucky ones who still had a job, but I was still stony broke. A pint was only about thirty pence, but I literally didn't have a penny to my name. 'Sorry mate,' I said. 'Totally skint.'

'Don't worry about it, lads, I'll sort yous out,' said the Swerve. He bent down as if to tie his shoelace, lifted a flap on his trainers, and ceremonially produced an immaculately crisp ten-pound note. It looked like he'd ironed it. 'Always got to have an emergency tenner, lads,' he said with a big smile. 'Come on. Central Bar, here we come.'

That was us on the piss for the day. That ten quid bought us thirty pints.

On other occasions, we'd meet up with other mates and they'd buy us food or beer. That was just how it was in those days. We looked after each other and shared whatever we had. What was yours was everyone's. You couldn't exist in that environment if you were tight with money. You could start the day with nothing but still manage to get bevvied, buy a takeaway and pay for a taxi ride home, because all your mates would chip in to help you out.

I loved that camaraderie. After a big night out, Mum would

come into my room in the morning and say, 'Smells like a brewery in here.' She was probably right, because there would be four guys sleeping on the floor. And downstairs there would be broken eggs all over the kitchen floor from the fry-up we'd tried to make when we'd rolled in half-cut the night before. That's just the way I am. I need to be around people. I've always been like that from a very young age, when I used to have wee pals over for sleepovers. I hate being on my own for long. I like people; I'm interested in people. So that environment was perfect for me – spending time with like-minded people who worked hard, played hard and lived life to the full. I also liked the macho element of it. I'd played football, but I'd never played rugby or been in the cadets. This was the first time I was mixing with men and I was learning from them all the time – learning about life. It was a great thing.

Many of those lessons took the form of practical jokes. Once, at Brize Norton, gentle giant Bucket-of-Shite came burling in and tried to open his locker. But I'd switched the padlock earlier in the day. He was cursing and swearing as he tried to open the door. Eventually I said, 'See you, you daft fucker, here,' switched his key for the right one, and let him open it. But when he did, he discovered the second part of the joke – I'd removed all the contents, too. He went mental while the rest of us rolled about laughing.

The classic one involved the barracks' bunk beds. They had

metal frames, with the springs in the middle hooked over eyelets. Bucket-of-Shite used to think he was great and would come bounding in, leap in the air and land flat on his back on the bed. So one day we undid all the springs, arranged the mattress so it looked perfect, and then watched him fall straight through and go splat on the ground.

One time, Bucket-of-Shite, Dougie Craig and myself went down to Brize Norton for cannon-fodder training. At that time, there were three TA paratroop battalions: 15 Para, which was based in Scotland; 10 Para, which was London; and 4 Para, which was the rest of England, more or less. We were jumping every day, but these other lads were going through training and knew they wouldn't jump until the Thursday. So they were getting pissed up every night, coming in late, waking us up, being general dicks. We had to be up early every morning, and we had no money till later in the week, so we were raging with these new boys. Every night, Dougie would sing out to them, 'Wait till Wednesday ... wait till Wednesday.' They'd say, 'Fuck off, you Jock bastards!' and it would go on all night. But we got paid on the Wednesday, and we didn't have to jump the next morning. Now it was our turn. We went out on the piss and Dougie – who was even smaller than me – came charging into the barracks after midnight and flicked on all the lights. 'It's fucking Wednesday boys!' he shouted at the top of his voice and tipped them all out of their beds. We had them up all night. *All* night. Since we were para trained, they couldn't mess with us, and revenge was sweet.

A little while later, my papers finally came through and I travelled down to Aldershot, the regular Parachute Regiment depot. When I left home, everyone told me not to forget where I came from – to be proud of my background in the TA Paras, Dundee and Scotland. The Queen and Country thing didn't really work on us Scots, and it was the same for the Taffs and Paddies. We did it for ourselves, our own countries, *esprit de corps*, our mates. That is basically how the British Army, and every other army, operates. Tribalism is everything. We ate together, slept together, shat together, fought together. The buddy system means you're prepared to do everything for each other, including die. Guys charge into machine-gun nests and probable death for their mates, not for Queen and Country. You do everything with a buddy, you depend on each other. If one is asleep, the other is awake; if one has the front, the other covers the rear. You share the burden, the camaraderie and the teamwork.

That system runs right through the entire army: British Army–Parachute Regiment–battalions–companies–platoons–sections–buddies. It is a tried and tested formula that works. If that reliance on those around you ever broke down, then the whole army would break down, too.

There were about sixty of us new boys, but only eighteen had come straight from Civvy Street. The rest of us were either ex-TA or boy soldiers who had been in since they were sixteen. I had so much respect for those who had come straight from Civvy Street. They had never worn boots in their life and were brand new to the army. Guys like me, who had come from the TA, were expected to help them through. If the junior officers came into our room and our stuff was in good order while the new guys' kit looked like shit, it would be us who got it in the neck, not them, because we should know better. That made us work as a team. It's how the British Army operates. You must always remember that you're only as strong as your weakest member.

I decided early on to keep a low profile, play the grey man. There was no way I was going to stick my head above the parapet and get picked on. But that's not to say I was allowed to cruise through, either. Like all the other TA guys, I was expected to pitch in and help the Civvy Street lads. In spite of our best efforts, though, the attrition rate among them was huge. They dropped out left, right and centre, unable to hack the physical stuff and the discipline. That was never an option for me. I knew I couldn't go back to Dundee without a red beret. I would've been ashamed. So no matter how bad it got, I knew I would never give up.

Strict professionalism in all aspects of army life was critical to creating a crack force. On exercise, we would always collect our rubbish and take it back to base with us, eroding all evidence of us ever having been there. If I saw a crisp packet or sweet wrapper left behind, I knew it would have been left by a crap-hat – the name we gave to any soldier who was not one of us, who was not a Para. If we did the same thing, the punishment was severe. And if you walked a yard away from your weapon, you were in the shit. When you were running up a hill, you were forced to go through intense pain. On a map-reading exercise, you couldn't be nearly right – you had to be spot on. In combat, it could mean life or death. As a para, you have to be self-sufficient. When you're dropped behind enemy lines, as they were at Arnhem in the Second World War, you have to sustain yourself and survive until the support reaches you.

We were expected to know the history of the regiment. It was a young regiment by British Army standards, only dating back to 1941, but it had won a lot of battle honours in that time. In the depot, all the blocks where we stayed were named after VC winners, and you had to learn all their names. Meanwhile, the battalion barracks up the hill were named after battle honours. If you were on parade and the sergeant major asked who such-and-such was, you had better know. You needed to know everything – what the colours meant, dates, names. They really instilled it in you. The history of the regiment was a big thing.

The main difference between being in the TA and the regulars was the amount of time we spent doing bullshit in the full-time army. We always seemed to be cleaning the toilet blocks. We were even forced to boot-polish the toilet seats! Even though there were six cubicles, four would be cleaned and were not to be used each day. You never got much bullshit, or even much down time, as a weekend soldier because you had to cram so much learning into such a short period of time. But now we had to make bed blocks, so the sheets and blanket formed a perfect cube, like a double-decker sandwich. It was a right pain in the arse – so much so that guys used to sleep on the floor so they wouldn't have to make up their bed block every morning. Other guys bought extra blankets and sheets from the local army supply store and made up one that was perfect all the time, then they just sat it on their beds for inspection. But if you got caught doing that, you would be in the shit. I've seen whole wardrobes thrown out of windows because something wasn't quite right with them. That would be the end of your plans for a night out. Suddenly that privilege would be removed – and not just from you, but from the whole group of lads. Everybody suffered because of you. That made you sharpen up fast, because you would be fucking despised by all the other lads. The army's all about building teamwork and camaraderie, and instilling discipline. If they say jump, you ask, 'How high?'

Attention to detail gave us confidence, belief in our abilities, an aura that we were unbeatable. We were the fittest, strongest and toughest, but it was the mental training that really gave us the edge. Belief in the training would get us through. It was basic psychology, but it worked. Strive for perfection, always improve. It doesn't matter how good you are. When Linford Christie was the fastest man on the planet, he still had a coach. He still had to train every day, with countless track sessions, getting out of the blocks quicker, lifting weights, dietary constraints, striving to improve or else someone would soon overtake him. The best business people in the world have life coaches. People around them improve, so they can't stand still. It's very much the same in the paras. Going through the pain, putting in the extra mile, developing the ability to go without sleep for three days instead of two were all crucial, because when it came to it, we knew we could handle anything that was put in front of us.

The paras are the best troops in the British Army, with many going on to join the elite SAS. The marines are second best. That rivalry between the marines and us was always there, but there was also a begrudging respect between the two. There was that ancient feeling that you get when two tribes go to war – like when Scotland play England at rugby or Celtic and Rangers play a football match. We respected them, but we still wanted to beat them. And we knew that they were the real deal. They were well-trained, proper soldiers, just like us. We would never call a marine a crap-hat. We might call him a cabbage-head or a prick, but never a crap-hat.

For a lad from Dundee, Aldershot is a long way from home. It's the south of England, next stop France. Naturally, I gravitated to other Scots – we tend to find each other – but I never felt homesick. I was too busy for that. Whenever a new recruit from Scotland came in, they were directed towards me and my mates. It was a natural thing to look after your own – tell them what to do, what not to do, share kit around. It was good to see Ally Melvin again, he came down shortly after me and we palled up. But I had a lot of other good mates in 2 Para who weren't Scots, especially Dave Parr from Lincolnshire, who would later be tragically killed in the Falklands. Another pal was Wayne 'Taff' Rees, a rugby-mad Valleys boy. He was a fit, handsome bloke – good with the women. I remember coming back to the barracks after a Saturday afternoon drinking session and finding Taff sitting propped up on his bed. 'What the fuck's wrong with you?' I asked.

'Oh man, it's my neck,' he said, rolling his head around his shoulders. 'It's killing me. Did it at rugby and the hospital told me to exercise it.'

It turned out he had a broken spine and was nearly paralysed.

Then there were the brothers 'Wing' and 'Wang' Hanley. They were totally different characters, absolute polar opposites. Wang was always in the shit, always landing himself in the army jail, while Wing – who ended up in the SAS – was straight down the line, a real professional, ambitious, always doing weights, training.

Everyone had a nickname, but I managed to escape copping a bad one. Of course, I was called Banksy or Jock, but I just didn't respond to any other moniker they tried to stick on me. They should've called me 'Teflon' because their daft nicknames never stuck, thankfully.

The Jocks mainly hung around with the Welsh and the Northerners. We were all a long way from home, so while the local lads from London and the South-East could go and visit their families and girlfriends at the weekend, we were forced to stay put. As a result, we got very close. We were on the piss together each week and strong bonds grew. We'd hit the bevvy with the others occasionally, but there was very much a natural divide, even though everyone was tolerated and generally got on OK.

The training was good, and even enjoyable in a perverse kind of way. I knew it was the real deal, the toughest of the tough, and that appealed to me. We went on exercises in our eight-man sections – corporal, lance-corporal and six guys – each of which worked as a wee team within the platoon, and we were all given roles. I was number-two on the 'Gimpy' – the 7.62mm General Purpose Machine Gun (GPMG) – so my main job was to carry all the ammunition and make sure we never ran out. My other task was to replace the barrel when it got white-hot after a lot of use.

Finally, after twenty-six weeks of hard graft, I was through. My passing-out parade was held at Aldershot. The army always knew I wanted to join 2 Para, known as the 'Scottish Battalion'. It was not all Jocks, but most of us ended up there.

The corporal who took me through training was in 1 Para, and when we were getting ready for the parade it was his job to dish out the different-coloured lanyards – red for 1 Para, blue for 2 Para, green for 3 Para. When my turn came, he said, 'Banks, 1 Para.'

I was mortified. 'I'm not going,' I said stubbornly.

He threw the red lanyard at me and told me I had no choice. 'You *are* going, Banks. You're in 1 Para. I've claimed you.'

'You what? How can you "claim" me? I'm not going.'

All the other corporals were there, watching me getting more and more wound up, blood rising, fists clenched, digging my feet in and shaking my head.

'I'm not going,' I repeated.

Then they all burst out laughing and threw me my blue lanyard. I felt such a dick, but very relieved.

My parents drove down for the passing-out ceremony and stayed in a local hotel. It was a fantastic day. We had practised our marching and shined everything up to the hilt. The band was playing, Mum was taking pictures, it was great. At the meal afterwards the staff came over and spoke with the families. It was the proudest moment of my life.

I had really loved the training, all of it. But once I had passed out, a realisation hit me that I'd just trained for a job that I would never do. I really believed that. There was no war on the horizon. There was Northern Ireland, of course, and we had just lost eighteen guys at Warrenpoint, but that was a different sort of fight.

I joined 2 Para's D Company in September 1981. I had been in the battalion only a couple of weeks when I went to bed half-pissed and got battered in the night. Two guys from B Company came in armed with metal mugs and proceeded to bash me about the head. The room contained eight beds, with a small room off where our lance-corporal slept. Unfortunately for my attackers, he wasn't out that night and came in and caught them. But by then I had already been bashed unconscious. I was taken to hospital where I was kept under observation for a day.

My platoon was massively pissed off. Even though I was a new kid, the attack felt like an attack on everyone, especially as it was by guys from another company. So in the end it worked out well for me and helped me to be accepted by the others. The guys who did it were bang to rights and their careers were over. They spent months in Colchester Jail awaiting court martial, and then they were kicked out. All that training and suffering for nothing. And in the early 1980s it wasn't easy to find a new job on Civvy Street.

Just after I had recovered from the bashing I went on my first exercise – out to Kenya for six weeks. It was a real adventure, flying out of Brize Norton in DC-10s with the whole battalion. I was still the new boy, so I had to keep a reasonably low profile. It wasn't like going to Germany, which wasn't that different from the UK. This was Africa – it was exotic and amazing. The atmosphere in the battalion was different, too. In Aldershot, the rules were the rules, there was no leeway, and the old brass tossers were always looking on. But once we were away, things relaxed a bit.

We stayed at a place called Archer's Post, which they reckon is one of the hottest places on earth. I can attest to that, because at one point I collapsed through heat exhaustion while lugging the Gimpy tripod on my shoulders. Jungle and desert training was hard for all of us – the noise, heat, humidity, bugs, carrying loads of kit up muddy hills. Even the senior officers found it tough, especially trying to read a map in the jungle, where everything looks the same so it's easy to become disorientated. Camping in the jungle was a very strange experience for me. I would get bivvied up at night, go to sleep and wake in terrible sweats from really vivid dreams, like getting trampled by elephants. The only time I've experienced anything similar is on skiing holidays, when sometimes I dream of skiing over cliffs.

We had done live firing in training on the Brecon Beacons, but our exercises out in Africa were on a much larger scale, a real sight to behold. The artillery would boom in, aircraft would screech overhead and missiles would be firing in all directions. It was the first time I had seen how a full battalion could operate and it was truly impressive, not to mention quite scary.

We stayed in tented encampments, and the local kids would run around, wide-eyed at us funny-looking white chaps, trying to flog us crap or get their hands on free shit, shouting, 'Biscuit, Johnny? Biscuit, Johnny?' Typical squaddies, we used to throw them hexi blocks – solid fuel for the stove cookers – and crack up laughing when they tried to eat them. Or we would get a scorpion, break up a hexi block and make a ring of fire around it, and watch it sting itself to death. I cringe about it now. It was so cruel. But to bored young squaddies, it was great fun.

We had two choices where to go during our R&R time: Mombasa or Lake Naivasha, a freshwater lake in the Great Rift Valley. I decided to try to save some money, so I swerved

Mombasa and headed to the lake, which was boring as hell. I soon got sick of looking at hippos, and I was even more pissed off when the guys who'd been to Mombasa came back raving about the beaches, the bars and the women. The one place where we could go drinking was at Nanyuki, a wee market town that had a sportsman's bar. It's still there, apparently, and squaddies still visit it, still pick up women, and still contract venereal diseases – only they're much more deadly now.

Just before I went up to Dundee for my Easter leave my sergeant major, Nobby Clarke, told me I would have to interrupt my leave to come back for the court martial of the two pricks who had beaten me up.

When I got back to Aldershot I noticed that a number of the officers and senior NCOs had returned and were busy making preparations for what I would later learn would be our departure. After I gave my evidence Nobby Clarke asked me what my plans were.

I told him, 'I'm going back to Dundee to finish my leave.'

He replied, 'Probably wouldn't bother if I was you. We are just going to call everyone back.'

He didn't tell me any more, and I didn't take his advice. I took that bloody train all the way to Dundee, but my dreams of yet more drunkenness and debauchery came to nothing. The minute I got home, Mum presented me with a telegram.

It read simply 'Bruneval' – the name of my barracks and the codeword that meant I had to return to Aldershot right away. I had just got off the bloody train.

Aw nawww, I thought. Surely we're not really going to fight the fucking Argies, are we?

CHAPTER 3

GOOSE GREEN

The balloon was going up.

Mum was worried. 'Is there going to be a war?' she asked. 'I hope not.'

I reassured her: 'Don't worry. It won't come to anything. A bit of bluster and a show of force, most likely. The politicians will sort it out.' Then I caught the next train south. I didn't even have time to unpack my kit-bag.

How wrong I was. Maggie Thatcher was going to have one last roll of the imperial dice and we were going to fight in Britain's first conventional war since Korea, thirty years before. But back at Aldershot, we still didn't believe it would ever happen. The Argentinians – already dubbed 'Argies' in the jingoistic British press – would back down and the Yanks, who pretty much ran South America, would force out Galtieri.

The Argies were unlucky with their timing. The Royal Navy had just completed a major exercise, so they were all set up to put together a massive task force quickly. As the elite troops of the British Army, we knew we would be in the forefront of any action, and sure enough 2 and 3 Para were both selected to sail. (1 Para were on Arctic training in Norway at the time and would later be taunted as 'the chosen frozen' for missing the war.)

The newspapers and television news bulletins were full of reports on the Falklands, with images of Governor Rex Hunt wearing a plumed helmet like something out of Gilbert and Sullivan – a relic of a bygone era. But they gave me the chance to learn what it was all about. Britain had occupied the islands, which lay 300 miles off the coast of Argentina, in 1833 after various other nations had laid claim to them. They were about the size of Wales and had previously been claimed by France, Spain and Argentina itself, as well as the British, who had first established a colony in the 1760s. Clearly, many people thought these remote islands were significant. When the sinews of British industry were greased by whale oil, the Falklands were an important whaling station. Then, when the Royal Navy switched from sail to steam power, the islands were a key coaling station that served to extend the navy's worldwide reach. There had even been an important battle there during the First World War, with the British scoring a morale-boosting naval victory over the Germans in 1914.

The locals were known as 'kelpers' because of the abundance of seaweed around the rocky coastline. About three-quarters of the two thousand kelpers, who made their living from sheep farming, were of British descent – most of them Welsh or Scottish in origin. The remainder were of Chilean or Argentinian descent, but apparently they all spoke with West Country or Cornish accents, and none of them had a hankering to live under a dictatorship that thought it was perfectly acceptable to murder the left-wing mothers of new-born babies and then hand the children over to loyal fascist families for adoption.

Galtieri was one of a motley crew of South American dictators who had been installed by the Yanks or were kept in power by them because the Americans were terrified of left-wing, pro-Castro regimes in their own backyard. Some of these dictators morphed into psychopathic tyrants who spent decades butchering and torturing their own people. Galtieri had been Argentinian dictator Jorge Videla's right hand man for a few years in the seventies before seizing power himself in 1981. (In 2010, Videla was tried for crimes against humanity, found guilty, and sentenced to life imprisonment.) A drunkard and an opportunist, Galtieri had run a much-feared death squad known as Battalion 601. During Argentina's so-called 'Dirty War', it had played a major role in the torture, murder and disappearance of some 30,000 citizens, many of whom were flung alive out of planes into the murky brown waters of the River Plate. The Americans had turned a blind eye to this, and then courted and aided Galtieri when he came to power, but they soon realised that he was a Frankenstein's monster whom they could not control.

By 1982, Argentina was an exhausted, fractured and divided society. The locals could agree on only one thing – the Falklands belonged to them. They should be regained for Argentina and renamed the Malvinas. Galtieri sensed an opportunity to stem the increasing domestic opposition to his regime and sent eight hundred commandos on to the islands on 2 April. Thousands more Argie troops followed, and the islanders were placed under house arrest. There was an out-pouring of joy in the streets of Buenos Aires and Galtieri claimed a great victory.

In Britain, though, Maggie Thatcher was having none of it. Within three days of the invasion, the vanguard of the task force had set sail and word soon came through that we would be next. As usual, our official British Army kit was crap – out-dated and not up to the job – so the army and navy stores in Aldershot did a roaring trade over the next seven days, with

Mum and Dad on their wedding day – they both came from humble Dundee backgrounds. (Tony Banks)

With my Mum in Cyprus where my dad was stationed with the RAF. (Tony Banks)

Me in my Sunday best. (Tony Banks)

My older brother Roddy, sister Terry and me, the youngest. (Tony Banks)

On holiday in Greece.
(Tony Banks)

On holiday in Greece with Gary Whyte – his death while serving with the French Foreign Legion affected me deeply. (Tony Banks)

Proud Paras. Posing with our much-coveted and newly-won red berets at our base in Aldershot. I am front row, second from the right.
(Tony Banks)

Taking a break from exercises in the tropics with my mates in D Company 2 Para.
(Tony Banks)

Picture taken during a break while on patrol in Belize.
(Tony Banks)

British troops surrender to Argentinian troops, 2 April 1982. (Press Association)

For the young Argentinian soldiers 'liberating the Malvinas' was the proudest day of their lives. Here a group pose with a captured British flag, Port Stanley. Omar Tabarez is kneeling, centre, with trumpet. (Omar Tabarez)

Cbo 1ro OMAR RENE TABAREZ
Banda Militar RI 25

Corneta de Orden del RI 25 que participa en el desembarco y
recuperación de las ISLAS MALVINAS, siendo el primero
en ejecutar Marcha Regular para izar por primera vez
Nuestro Pabellón en ese suelo.

Omar Tabarez playing his trumpet
as a soldier. He sounded the last
post for his dead comrades and was
traumatised by his war experiences.
(Omar Tabarez)

As the smallest in the regiment I am
easy to spot in the back row in this
2 Para group shot onboard the
Norland on our way to the Falklands.

We were steaming south to the South Atlantic when the *Belgrano* was sunk on 2 May 1982 with 321 lives lost. We realised then that the war was for real. (Getty Images)

Argentina strikes back – blasted remains of HMS *Sheffield*, hit on 4 May, being towed outside the exclusion zone. (Press Association)

San Carlos Bay – known to us as Blue Beach. We feared a D-Day style landing here but we were unopposed – thank God. (Press Association)

We were perched up in the Sussex mountains protecting the bridgehead, which was established on 21 May at San Carlos Bay. (Press Association)

guys spending fortunes stocking up with Australian ponchos and Norwegian fleeces, anything to make life more comfortable.

Having hit the shops during the day, we would hit the bars of Aldershot every night, thinking we would be leaving the next day. But our embarkation kept being put back. One day we were told we would be leaving from Hull, then it was off, then it was back on. Finally, we were trucked down to Portsmouth. The requisitioned North Sea car ferry we were to sail on did not look very warlike. Apart from a heli-deck, which had been welded on to the superstructure at the rear of the ship, it looked like we might have been going on a booze-cruise to Calais.

There was a real carnival atmosphere on 26 April when we boarded the MV *Norland*. Similar scenes must have been played out a thousand times in British military history, and we felt like we were creating our own bit of history, too. We were as proud as Punch as we walked up the gangplank. A military band was playing cheerful tunes like 'A Life on the Ocean Wave', and cheering crowds of supporters and family members were waving Union Flags. The docks were bedecked with red, white and blue bunting, and the world's press was there to report it all. It was very emotional and a bit surreal. As paras, we had been trained to go to war in the dead of night, boarding aircraft on military bases to make the most of the element of surprise, yet here we were, getting on a car ferry in broad daylight with fucking bands playing!

Thatcher made sure a real song and dance was made of us leaving, no doubt hoping to scare the Argies into backing down. We thought it was all a bit of a joke. After all, there was no threat to the UK, no threat to our loved ones. If we fought the Argentinians at all, it would be on the other side of the world. But I felt even that was unlikely. By the time we got halfway down there, to the Azores maybe, I reckoned we would be called back. So I just enjoyed the moment, being the centre of attention. We were in the headlines and were being recognised for something, which was great. It felt like a big jolly.

As we sailed out, the news came in that South Georgia had been retaken the previous day by a mixed SAS and SBS force. All the penguins and sheep on the island, a long-abandoned whaling station, were now free to live their lives as British citizens once again. The victory seemed to have been won easily. Britain had shown a bit of muscle and got the results. We had captured an Argie submarine too, the *Santa Fe*, so that was one less of them for us to worry about. Three Argies had been killed and one of the prisoners was Lieutenant Alfredo Astiz, wanted by France for the torture and murder of two French nuns during the Dirty War. Nice people, these Argies, I thought. But mostly the news just reinforced our opinion that we'd be back home as soon as we'd shown a little force.

Once the euphoria of our send-off had evaporated, we settled down to our month-long voyage cooped up on a car ferry. The bosses knew they had to keep us busy. Fortunately, the army is great at that, because when soldiers get bored they tend to start punching lumps out of each other. We were trained killers and here we were, with all of that pent-up aggression, living in very confined quarters. There was limited space for physical training, but we made the most of what we had. We did laps of the car decks carrying our buddies on our shoulders, lots of sprints, press-ups and sit-ups. There were plenty of competitions too, between platoons and sections: tug-of-war, sprint relays, anything to keep us occupied. The battalion even organised a sports day. We played a pretty aggressive form of deck hockey and did bayonet drill. And we spent lots of time doing target practice – throwing bags of rubbish from the stern and blasting them, making sure our self-loading rifles and Gimpys were zeroed in.

More ominously, we also had constant first-aid and medical training. Thankfully, there was no threat of either chemical or nuclear warfare, so we didn't concentrate on that. Most of our instruction was about ABC – airways, breathing, circulation. Our buddies were our practice dummies. Everyone carried morphine and a drip, and we were shown how to find a vein and get a needle in. Failing that, we were instructed to shove the tube up the injured bloke's arse, just to get the medication and painkillers into him. I've no idea if it would have worked, but that's what we were told. They also showed us how to use bandages and how to reduce blood loss. But they never showed us how to deal with burns victims . . . and that would come to haunt us. By the end of the voyage, we knew exactly what to do with gunshot wounds and even with guys who had been blown up, but we had no idea what to do with guys who were on fire, burning flesh falling off them, their charred skin hanging from them like ribbons. Nevertheless, all our training certainly saved a lot of lives. During the conflict, 2 Para recorded an incredibly low death rate among the wounded.

We also spent a lot of time in the classroom, learning about the Argies' military capabilities. We were told they had a lot of conscripts, but these were supported by a quite well-trained and disciplined regular force. So we had to be prepared for a formidable enemy who had been on the islands for weeks and was well dug-in. Intelligence officers gave us briefings on their firepower, the names of their planes and tanks, and so on. Then, after class, we would read books and learn more details on each plane – how to identify them, their weapons, range, top speed. I swotted up on their Skyhawks, Mirages, Super Etendards, Pucaras and Aermacchi 339s. For an army which had not fought a war since the 1870s, when it had launched a 'Conquest of the Desert' to stamp out Indian raiders in Patagonia, and which had spent decades organising coups and fighting its own people, it certainly had an amazing array of aircraft and weaponry. In fact, their equipment was superior to ours in many respects. But at least our intelligence was very thorough. We even knew how many armoured personnel carriers they had. As we left one briefing, one of the guys said, 'Fucking hell. I bet they even know the colour of Galtieri's underpants.'

'Well, we know what colour they're *gonna* be,' somebody responded.

When the laughter had died down, I couldn't help wondering, 'If we're so bloody clever, how were they able to take us by surprise in the first place?'

To kill time, most of us played cards, gambled and read books, but some became a bit philosophical – writing poetry and thinking deep thoughts. I spent hours poring over my kit, making sure I knew where everything was, chucking out stuff that was unnecessary, anything surplus to the most basic requirements. Paras routinely get their ration boxes and bin half of it, because you do not want to carry the weight. We weren't ferried about in armoured personnel carriers, we tabbed everywhere, with everything we required on our backs, so keeping the weight down was critical. As usual, a lot of us had supplied our own kit, something the young guys in

Iraq and Afghanistan were still having to do twenty and thirty years later.

The boat was cramped and boring, but we were well fed and kept ourselves fit. We were allowed two cans of beer each per night. But a platoon of thirty guys would nominate a few guys every evening and hand all the allocation over to them, which meant everyone had a few chances to get blootered during the month-long trip. When the orderly officers came round, they couldn't understand why a handful of guys were absolutely steaming. There were plenty of crazy scenes of guys running around the ship, completely off their heads.

I bunked with my mate 'Rocky' Hudson. He was six foot four and took the top bunk. All five foot six of me was underneath. We used to roll about laughing for no reason at all. We joked about Argie subs about to torpedo us. It was really dark, gallows humour, but it kept us going. Rocky was a Londoner, and while he wasn't your typical East End barrow boy, you could never tell whether he was telling you the truth or lying through his teeth. In Aldershot, he would head off to London for the weekend and come back with these great tales of shagging. I never found out if they were true. He was a good-looking blond bloke who always had women around him, but he was tough to pin down. He wasn't a hard man, not a fighter. More of a nice guy. Still, it was always a good idea to have a big mate, as he might be prepared to carry a bit of extra weight.

We ploughed on, and the sea seemed to get rougher the further south we went. Despite the best efforts of the hierarchy, boredom eventually became a problem, but we managed to defeat it with the help of an unlikely hero. Among the crew on the *Norland* was a gay steward who would become a 2 Para icon. He was a big, round-shouldered guy, larger than life, and camper than any row of tents ever pitched in the history of the British Army. At first, he got dog's abuse – every kind of homophobic insult ever invented and quite a few that were invented especially for him. But he just smiled and took it all in his stride. We called him 'Bendy Wendy', which eventually evolved into 'Wendy'. In turn, he called us his 'boys'.

Gradually, he won us over. He looked after us, made sure we were OK, and got extra rations for us. In fact, all of the ship's staff were incredible. They were all volunteers and didn't need to be serving on a ship that had been commandeered by the Royal Navy, so we all respected them greatly for that. But Wendy was more than a brave volunteer – he turned out to be a great entertainer. He was brilliant on the piano and every night in the forward lounge he would hold sing-songs which became legendary affairs and played a big part in keeping up our spirits. I'm sure a few of the guys got their rocks off with him.

In spite of Wendy's best efforts, though, I became ever more desperate to get off that ship. We weren't sailors, we were paratroopers. Scuffles broke out, with tensions running high. A load of fit, young guys caged up on a ship are eventually going to beat the shit out of each other. And the mountainous seas that pounded the roll-on, roll-off ferry hardly helped the situation, especially for the unlucky ones who came down with seasickness. I would walk out of my cabin and lean on the handrail to take it all in. The grey seas rose to the grey heavens to create a depressing wall of greyness. Sometimes the container ship *Atlantic Conveyor*, which was following us, would momentarily disappear from sight. Its decks were laden with most of our helicopters, including the Chinooks that were our workhorses and would lift us into battle. Funny, I thought. All those choppers on one ship. Talk about all your eggs in one basket.

But the complacent mood aboard the *Norland* changed suddenly with one piece of news. On 2 May, the British submarine HMS *Conqueror* sank an Argentinian battleship. The *General Belgrano*, an ancient ex-US Navy vessel that had survived the Japanese attack on Pearl Harbor, had gone down with massive loss of life – 321 Argentinian sailors had died. The Argentinian Navy was effectively knocked out of the war and it never left harbour again. We were impressed by the sinking of the *Belgrano*, but the news was not greeted by cheering or anything like that. Instead, it brought home to us that this war was real. The situation was escalating and there would be no going back.

Two days later came even more sobering and shocking news. I can remember the hairs on the back of my neck literally standing up when I heard it. Argie planes had struck back and attacked a British Type 42 destroyer, HMS *Sheffield*, with French-made missiles. We had never heard the name of the weapon before, but from that moment on it would haunt the whole task force. It was a massive wake-up call. The Argies had Exocet missiles – lethal weapons over a range of forty-five miles with ferocious destructive power. The *Shiney Sheff*, as it was known, had formed part of our defensive screen, but its Sea Dart missiles had proved no match for the surface-skimming Exocets. Twenty men died in the attack, while many of the survivors were badly burned and wounded. As they waited for rescue, they kept up morale by singing the Monty Python hit 'Always Look on the Bright Side of Life'.

The atmosphere on the *Norland* became much more tense. The joviality stopped. The training became more focused. We were ordered to sharpen our bayonets. I did so intently, but as I hunched over, grinding away at the cold steel, I could not help thinking that it was a bizarre, almost medieval ritual at the end of the twentieth century. From then on, I studied the Argentinian aircraft and weaponry as if my life depended on it. My alertness reached a new level. I was determined to do whatever was necessary to survive.

I had never really been a practising Catholic, but my faith must have been buried somewhere deep inside me because now, faced with possible death, I started attending mass. There were not many of us Catholics on the ship, maybe just thirty or forty, but they included our gifted second-in-command, Major Chris Keeble, who was very devout and carried his own prayer book with him.

We stopped at Freetown in Sierra Leone to take on supplies and put the women crew members ashore. The rest of us stayed on board, and soon we were sailing on to Ascension Island. When we arrived, 3 Para were waiting for us aboard the *Canberra*, the P&O cruise ship which had been requisitioned by the Ministry of Defence. It was sitting in the shadow of sheer volcanic mountains that rose out of the Atlantic. We spent some time practising helicopter airlifts off the ship in preparation for our invasion, then the *Canberra* joined our convoy and we sailed on.

The British propaganda machine made sure that the Argentinian invaders knew that the UK's crack troops – the SAS, the Parachute Regiment, the Royal Marine Commandos, the Scots Guards, the Welsh Guards and the dreaded Gurkhas – were all coming to get them and we meant business. Unknown to us, the ferocious reputation of the diminutive Nepalese hillmen – and especially their skill with their curved *kukri* killing knives – was already having a big impact on the morale of the freezing and poorly fed Argentinian conscripts who were waiting for us.

Now there were regular alerts over the PA system, warning us that Argentinian submarines were in the vicinity. We would be sent to lie on our beds and put on our lifejackets and helmets. I used to question these orders, asking all and sundry, 'What the fuck use is this going to be against a torpedo attack?' I always questioned the way things were done. But I always knew exactly how to get to a lifeboat, the quickest route, how I would do it. I'm still like that today: if I'm on a flight, I always know where the nearest exit is and plan for the worst.

One afternoon, sirens sounded and we dismissed it as yet another drill. But then a booming voice came over the tannoy, announcing, 'This is not a drill!' Bloody hell, it was the real thing. One of my mates shouted, 'The fucking Argies are gonna do a *Belgrano* on us.' That gave one of the platoon wits an opportunity to imitate Corporal Jones out of *Dad's Army*: 'Don't panic! Don't panic!' About three minutes later, we had cleared the boat stations and were wearing our steel helmets and lifejackets. We braced ourselves for torpedoes. A rumour went around that an Argentinian submarine was right beneath us. *Fucksake!* Then came the relief of the all-clear siren. It turned out that the sonar operators had mistaken a school of whales for a submarine. But those whales certainly focused all of our minds.

As we continued to head south, there was a change of plan. This came as a serious shock to the volunteer crew of the *Norland* and to us. We were not going to invade by helicopter after all. The powers-that-be had discovered that the *Norland* had side doors that were suitable for disembarkation on to landing craft. The captain and crew were told that their car ferry was to become an amphibious assault vessel! And the airborne elite of the British Army were to be ferried ashore by cabbage-heads! It was to be Britain's first amphibious landing since Suez in 1956.

Finally, on 21 May, almost a month since we had left Pompey, the engines fell silent and the *Norland* dropped anchor. Our convoy had slipped into San Carlos Bay, a deep-water channel on the north-east coast of East Falkland. The Argies had neglected to mine the channel and the steep hills around the bay rendered their Exocets ineffective. But we were still horrendously vulnerable to air attack. Ahead of us lay 'Blue Beach', the codename for the area that would form the bridgehead for the British landings. It had once hosted a mutton-freezing plant, and I told myself that there was no way I was going to end up as dead meat. We were camouflaged up and checked our gear for the hundredth time. I was determined to stay alert at all costs. I had brains and they would keep me alive. I wasn't going to rely on anyone else, especially not our platoon commander, Chris Waddington. He had 'won the sword' for being the best in his year at Sandhurst, but he pranced around like he was top boy. He was nicknamed the 'Boy Wonder'. Needless to say, he was not popular with the lads, not least because of his insistence on taking us out on attack training at the crack of dawn.

Most of the officers, especially the young ones, were public schoolboy prats as far as I was concerned. They were very different from us Toms. We called them 'Ruperts'. Most of the second lieutenants, including Waddington (who at nineteen was the same age as me), had come straight out of the factory and they knew jack shit about anything. But they still thought they could stroll in and automatically command our respect. Bollocks to that. They were naive young laddies, just like us, but they were from a different world. They were generally middle or upper class, while we were mostly working class. Class distinction was rife in the army back then. Still, the paras probably attracted the best of them, and we gave some of them grudging respect for not taking the easy option of joining some crap-hat regiment. That was not the case with Waddington, though.

Before we arrived at San Carlos Bay, our commanding officer, Lieutenant Colonel Herbert 'H' Jones, had given us a briefing outlining our role and explaining how we were going to get ashore. Then we were to take up positions on Sussex Mountain to protect the southern flank of 3 Commando Brigade, who would attack Port Stanley to the west. Our job was to bottle up a large force of Argies at a remote settlement called Goose Green. They had an airstrip down there and had imprisoned over a hundred villagers in the community hall. Jones was in his element addressing the troops and seemed to be relishing it. He was a tall, handsome Old Etonian and cut a dashing figure – a bit of a film star. He was not a hardcore para, though: he was a crap-hat, having joined the paras in 1979 after almost twenty years with the Devonshires. I sometimes thought he played up his reputation as an action man to compensate for being a crap-hat. But he had already fought and won a critical battle on our behalf. He had insisted that we must have double the normal number of Gimpys. The army bosses gave in and thank God they did.

Jones told us we were going to have the honour of being the first troops of the invasion force to land. Funny – it didn't feel like an honour! Diversionary raids had already been launched on the islands, and a false trail had been laid to suggest numerous landings elsewhere. But we didn't know whether the Argies had fallen for it. When Jones finished and we broke up, I noticed that the map he'd been using during the briefing was still stuck to the wall. I quickly swiped it. I thought it might be useful. I was already in survival mode. I must have been the only Tom on the island with a map. I carried it throughout the war in my Bergen rucksack.

I had my map, my wits about me and a wary eye on Waddington. I was as ready as I would ever be. While Waddington was a prick, I knew that the platoon sergeant and corporals were experienced guys. And the officer commanding our company, Major Phillip Neame, was absolutely brilliant. His father had won the Victoria Cross in the First World War and he seemed a natural leader of men. He was tough and resourceful, a keen mountaineer who had even climbed Mount Everest. But he managed to get up the noses of those above him, for instance by letting his hair grow too long. And I don't think he and Jones ever saw eye to eye. But his good judgement and cool professionalism would later prove crucial to our survival.

We were stuck down in the loading bay for hours, each of us tooled up with our gear. There wasn't much banter among the boys, and we became even more subdued when Padre Cooper piped up. He was well respected among the lads – not least because he was a crack shot and acted as a sniper instructor when he wasn't Bible-bashing. The bullet and the Bible – what a combination. The original Christian soldier. He had already taken the time to go round each section and have a chat to all of the men. Now he held a service. He grabbed our attention immediately by telling us, 'Look around you. Not everyone here is going to come back.' That had some of the guys, especially the married ones, swallowing hard.

We waited for the fleet of four landing craft in silence. Still, I was confident that if it came to it, we would be all right. We were told we were the elite, we had suffered a lot of blood, pain and beatings to get the beret, and we knew we had earned it. We were the shit. Around 70 per cent of the SAS was made up of paras, and we were ready to go to war. Not that I had any idea what was lying in wait for us. Almost none of us did. There was one Rhodesian guy in our battalion who had been in a full-scale conflict, but that was about it. The rest of us were quite naive, brainwashed by the British regimental system which had churned out top soldiers for centuries. Britain had punched well above its weight on the world stage for a long time, so they must have been doing something right. We knew we were professional soldiers, we had volunteered for this, and we had total confidence in our training and our leaders. We were fit and raring to go.

As the landing craft finally sidled alongside, there was a very British moment. The tannoy crackled into life and the tinny voice of the *Norland*'s captain thanked us for travelling with him and his crew and wished us a safe stay in the Falkland Islands. Talk about stiff upper lip! You would have thought he was dropping us off at Oostende for the weekend.

First we had to file to the cargo doors on the side of the ship. Then we had to make a leap for it on to the yawing landing craft, which were pitching up and down on the heavy swell – not easy when you have a pack that weighs as much as you do on your back. Some of the weight was made up of two 81mm high-explosive mortar bombs in plastic tubes that we had to drop off at designated points on our way inland for the mortar teams to pick up later. And I had the added burden of loads of ammo for the Gimpy, so making that leap was scary – much more frightening than jumping out of an aircraft. But we were desperate to get off that bloody ship, which any Argie aircraft could have turned into a flaming, floating coffin. As we began to pile out, one poor guy slipped and fell and got trapped between the ship and the landing craft. That delayed us even more. He survived but suffered a broken pelvis. It must have been agony. But he was a lucky bastard – it was the end of the war for him.

We didn't know if the beach landing would be opposed or unopposed, and that uncertainty was terrifying. A machine-gun nest might have been waiting to shred us all to pieces as soon as the ramp came down. It was like the D-Day landings at Normandy. Nearly two hundred of us were crammed in that bucket of a landing craft and we seemed to spend ages going around in circles. It was horrific. All of those jumps at Brize Norton and here we were invading by sea. This is mental, I thought. I've never even been on a landing craft and, to make matters worse, a cabbage-head is driving the boat. I hope the bastard gets us right up to the beach. I was at the very front of the landing craft, too. The Gimpy was our main firepower, so we had to get off first. Right in the line of fire. I would be the first to get it. Cold sweat trickled down my spine and my mouth dried. The atmosphere was expectant, nobody was speaking, and we did not even look at each other. We were all standing there as individuals, staring straight ahead, gathering our thoughts and our courage. When the landing craft shuddered to a stop and the ramp started to go down it was a moment of sickening vulnerability. But at least I couldn't hear any firing; just the whirr of the ramp and the gurgle of the engines. I prayed for a dry landing . . . and one without bullets.

The cabbage-head, to give him his due, got us right into the beach, so we had to run through only two or three inches of water. We stood still for a few moments, unsure what to do, until the cabbage-head started screaming at us to disembark. But we didn't understand his instructions – we were trained to jump out of planes to the word 'Go'. When it finally came from one of our officers, we didn't need any second invitations. We charged ashore, heads down, sprinting, expecting – *fearing* – the worst. There was no stopping to check if anyone was following. I knew they would be there. And there was no time to look up and see if the Argies were waiting for us – waiting for us to get closer before ripping us in half with their machine guns. Across the sand, up on to the track and our intended rendezvous point – still no fire. Unopposed. Thank *fuck*. We fell to the ground with our hearts racing, breathless with exhaustion and relief. I could have hugged that cabbage-head. We were home and nearly dry. Others weren't so lucky, though. They were dropped off in waist-deep, freezing water.

We tabbed south in the dark along the track and straight up the side of Sussex Mountain when dawn was breaking. We couldn't wait to get rid of the mortar bombs, which weighed 4.2 kilos each. We thought we had it tough ... until we saw the mortar guys. Those poor bastards were doubled over under the weight of their mortar plates, hardly able to walk. We scrambled up the steep slopes of the mountain, stumbling over tussocks of grass and through peat bogs. The ground was treacherously uneven and soaking wet. We were all wearing DMS boots, which looked the part – all shiny and posh. But they were basically made from compressed cardboard with a bit of leather stuck around them. My feet were like blocks of ice. When we got to the peak of Sussex Mountain, we collapsed on our backs, lying on our Bergens.

The plan was to dig-in to protect the bridgehead at San Carlos, but the hill was much like those in Scotland – bald, treeless and freezing cold – and we soon discovered that we couldn't dig trenches because the water table was too high. So we had to cut out soft, peaty bricks and build them up into sangars in front of our positions, like the walls of an igloo. Finally, Rocky and I were able to snatch a few hours' sleep. Exhausted by the effort and emotion of the landing, we huddled into our dug-out for protection from the howling wind, which felt like it was coming straight from Antarctica, and were soon out for the count.

The landings had been a success, with 2400 paras and marines getting ashore safely. The diversionary attacks had gone like clockwork, too. An SBS unit of twenty-five men had attacked Argie positions at Fanning Head, north of San Carlos Bay. With naval gunfire in support and using Gimpys, they easily defeated the sixty Argie defenders who refused to surrender. Eleven Argies were killed and six wounded. The rest escaped. To the south, the SAS attacked Argie positions at Darwin with such ferocity that the defenders thought they were under attack from an entire battalion.

But even though we had been unopposed at Blue Beach, we were not alone. The Argies had two special forces observers in place. They had watched our arrival and radioed back to base. Just as dawn broke, our attempt to snatch some rest was abruptly shattered. We leapt out of our skins with the sound of the sky being torn apart. Out of nowhere, Argie jets screamed overhead. We got down and trained our machine guns and rifles on them, but we looked at each other and frantically shouted in unison, 'What are the terms of engagement?' We could see the whites of the pilots' eyes, they were that low, but we didn't know if we could fire. Then a ship down below came under attack and opened up in reply. Eventually the order came and we opened up on the planes, too.

I looked down on San Carlos Bay and could see all our ships bobbing up and down – like sitting ducks. Soon we had a new name for our anchorage – Bomb Alley. The Argentinian pilots were incredibly skilful and very courageous. They flew in low over the water to avoid radar and surface-to-air missiles and were at the outer limits of their range. By the time they reached Bomb Alley, they had only two or three minutes to hit the first targets they saw. In the middle of the mayhem – with jets shrieking in, bombs exploding and anti-aircraft fire filling the air – we watched as the poor old *Norland* put about and steamed for safety. She was designed for day trips to Channel ports and here she was in the middle of a war zone. It was an echo of Dunkirk and she was lucky to escape unharmed.

Unbelievably, many of the bombs that were dropped on our ships had been made in Britain and sold to the Argies just a year earlier. Luckily for us, though, a lot of them failed to explode – not because of poor British workmanship but because the Argies were forced to drop them from such a low altitude. Later, it was reckoned we would have lost the war if half of the thirteen bombs that hit their targets and failed to explode had gone off. Also, because they had no time to select their targets, the Argies were unable to concentrate on our supply ships. If they had, they could have crippled us. Nevertheless, they were doing a lot of damage and men were dying in Bomb Alley.

These air raids were an incredible sight and became a daily routine. They produced an amazing adrenalin rush, too. This was for real. These bastards were trying to kill us. Every day, we sat on the side of the mountain and waited for the jets to come in and go for our ships. They knew those ships were our lifeline, the key to our success. We felt so sorry for the navy boys who just had to sit there – exposed on floating targets. We got to know when to expect the Argie jets. We knew their general flight paths, trajectories and even the rough time they would come over. Hunkered down in our shelters, bored out of our brains, we calculated that if it were such-and-such o'clock here, it must be dawn on the Argentinian mainland, and if they took off now and flew at such-and-such a speed, they would be here at such-and-such a time. When they arrived, we would all let loose and create an arc of fire six or seven aircraft lengths in front of the planes that they would have to fly through. The whole of San Carlos Bay would erupt with gunfire as we blazed away at them. Whenever we saw one go down, we were chuffed to bits. Paras don't go in for cheering – we leave the whooping and hollering to the Yanks – but we were well chuffed. We knew how many aircraft the Argentinian Air Force had, so we would congratulate ourselves, saying, 'Chalk off another Super Etendard, boys . . .'

There was continuous activity down on the beachhead. We could see supplies – ammunition, food, water and medicines – constantly brought ashore by ant-like figures. We all had to do our bit of guard – or stag – duty. It was four hours on and four hours off, when you were supposed to sleep. But no one did much more than catnap because it was so bloody cold. As usual, the British Army had provided us with useless supplies. Our long-johns were made of cotton, so once they were wet, they were freezing. Most of us had brought along women's tights, which were light and did the job much better. But some guys were soon going down with serious frostbite. The medics took away one poor bloke with toes which were completely black. (Strangely, the black guys' toes went white when they got frostbite.) Your boots were frozen on to your feet because they were so wet. I took off my socks and stuck them up in my groin, then Rocky and I faced each other and stuck our feet under each other's armpits. You would do anything to get warm. Big, tough men cuddled into each other. Others screamed out or whimpered because of the pain in their feet.

Our cardboard boots were claiming more casualties than any enemy action. And soon we were losing even more men to the misery of trench foot – even though the British Army had been well aware of the condition since 1914, when it afflicted thousands of soldiers in the trenches of the Western Front. It was a disgrace.

We could fire up the occasional brew with our little stoves and hexi blocks, but we had very limited drinking water, even though we were soaking wet. It was horrendous . . . and we hadn't even engaged in battle yet. By the end of our voyage, we had just wanted off that ship. Let's get this fucking job done, I'd thought. Let's get on with it. But now we were stuck on Sussex Mountain, freezing our nuts off. The five days we spent there were the longest of my life. I started to think that if it came down to a war of attrition eight thousand miles from home, we might well lose. The last war the British Army had fought in the southern hemisphere had been the Boer War, when we had narrowly averted disaster at the hands of a bunch of Afrikaner farmers. We couldn't let something like that happen here. We needed to move, to get on with what we were good at. We were ready to go and kill some Argie bastards.

Inevitably, before long, the moaners were coming out in force. We were all frustrated, but I tried to keep away from the whingeing bastards. They did my head in. Whingeing was a killer for morale, spreading like cancer, and I didn't need that. Life was miserable enough without having to hear how bad it was. The hills were utterly desolate, with their bleak and barren slopes scoured by a ceaseless and freezing wind that made it impossible for even the smallest tree to grow. Patches of gorse were the nearest thing to green in a khaki landscape. As we hunkered down to keep out of the wind whistling above our heads, boredom set in quickly and deeply. There was no banter, no cards, no games, no practical jokes. The food mainly consisted of hard-tack biscuits, tins of spam or bully beef and porridge or soup. Curry was everyone's favourite. It didn't really give us much pleasure, but it was still a highlight of the day. At least it was warm and heated up our insides. But cooking it was a pain in the arse, because it meant leaving our shelters to get water and then huddling around a wee fire, trying to keep the howling wind away from it.

And the last thing you wanted to do was go for a crap. That involved getting out of your gear and then hanging your arse out in plain view of everyone as you squatted over a hole in the ground. Being constipated seemed a much better option.

But at least we knew we wouldn't come under ground attack. We had the high ground, with clear views all around, and lots of firepower. The Argie jets weren't bothered with us much, either. We got an occasional strafing, which was terrifying, but it seemed to be no more than an afterthought. The pilots were really only interested in the ships, and they were making a lethal impact.

During our third night on the mountain, we were sitting around in the dark, trying to snatch some sleep and keep warm, when the peace was shattered by a terrific explosion. We all leapt to our positions, thinking we were being attacked. Everyone was called to stand-to and we were ready to go. Then we realised what had happened. We looked down into the darkness of Bomb Alley and saw a ship illuminated by a tremendous fireball and rocked by subsequent spectacular explosions of bright orange, purple and yellow. The air was filled with the smell of cordite and smoke. It was a terrible sight and my first thought was: Some poor bastard's had it. Someone must have been trying to defuse a bomb when it had gone up.

I didn't know it then, but we were watching the death throes of HMS *Antelope*. During the previous day, she had been hit by two 1100-pound bombs dropped by Skyhawk jets. They had killed one crewman on impact but had not exploded. After initial damage-control efforts, the *Antelope* had moved to more sheltered waters beneath us in the bay so that two bomb-disposal guys could defuse the bombs. They must have had nerves of steel and balls of titanium. The explosion that had woken us had occurred during the fourth attempt to defuse the second bomb – a delayed fuse had gone off and detonated it. Staff Sergeant James Prescott died instantly and Warrant Officer John Phillips, the other member of the team, was severely wounded. The ship was ripped open by the blast and a fire in the engine room soon spread. Five minutes after the commanding officer, Commander Nick Tobin, left the ship, the missile magazines began exploding. The explosions continued throughout the night, and the next day the *Antelope* was nothing but a twisted heap of molten metal.

The following day there was even more bad news. The *Atlantic Conveyor* was hit by two Exocets. Twelve men, including the ship's captain, Ian North, died and all but one of our Chinook helicopters were destroyed in the subsequent fireball. From now on, we knew we would be walking everywhere. But we were still longing to get into battle. We were cold, wet, miserable and just wanted to move – anything to get warmed up. And we were not the only ones keen for some action. The naval losses were bad news for the politicians, who were playing for high stakes. They wanted a morale-boosting victory on land – one that would stamp the British Army's ascendancy on the campaign – so it was decided to attack Goose Green. Some of the top brass argued against this, saying that the decision was made for political rather than strategic reasons and that the small Argie garrison posed little threat. But Colonel Jones was typically gung-ho and eager for battle.

So, after nearly a week of freezing our bollocks off, we were resupplied with ammo to replace what we had used having a pop at the Argie jets. Then, after a quick meal, we were ordered to get our fighting order together. That meant we could take nothing but our fighting kit – no Bergens, no sleeping bags. Just a bit of food and what we needed to fight. Being number two on the Gimpy, I carried only ammo, and I was loaded up with bullets. I had them everywhere – stuffed in my pockets, webbing and pack.

When we were ready, we started an overnight march towards Goose Green – a sheep-farming community that was the second-largest settlement in the Falklands. It was going to be a night attack in which we would enjoy the element of surprise. It would be short, sharp, vicious and very noisy – designed to throw the enemy into chaos. We needed the cover of darkness because there was no other kind of cover in that flat, barren landscape, and the Argies were well dug-in. They would be looking down from low hills across a narrow bottleneck that in daylight would have been a death-trap for us. The main line of their defence was strung between a place called Boca House, in the west, and Darwin Hill, in the east. Around three hundred Toms from 2 Para would advance over a mile-wide front and punch five miles deep to capture Goose Green. We would have artillery support from the commandos and the naval guns of HMS *Arrow*. We knew the locations of the Argie positions because the SAS had reconnoitred the area. What could possibly go wrong?

It would have been hard going even in daylight. But we were to descend the mountain and tab eleven miles in the middle of the night, when it was even more treacherous underfoot, with tussocky moongrass in invisible clumps. We marched along silently in single file, alone with our thoughts. But every now and then the silence was punctuated by a grunt or a groan as another guy tripped and sprained an ankle or fell into a bog. The moorland was one big mantrap. It was eerie, too. It felt like the hound of the Baskervilles could come bounding out of the darkness at any moment. Fuck knows what the Argies want this place for, I thought. It was a hellish slog, but we were all keyed up and ready to go into action. Then, inexplicably, after we had been tabbing for bloody hours, we were suddenly ordered to turn back. 'What the fuck is going on?' I wondered. 'Maybe the Argies have surrendered,' somebody suggested in a futile attempt to lighten our spirits. 'We'd be better off with the fucking Grand Old Duke of York in charge,' somebody else moaned through the darkness. We were completely pissed off and knackered. But not as pissed off as when we got back to where we had started only to be told to turn around and do it all over again! Typical army – couldn't organise a piss-up in a brewery, I thought. We had prepared for battle, got ourselves ready to survive whatever was coming, and then been let down. We were utterly and completely exhausted.

It transpired that not all of our helicopters had night-vision equipment, and those that did were busy dropping off SAS patrols. The choppers were to have brought up three light guns, to be positioned in an area near Camilla Creek House – a deserted shepherd's house three miles from Goose Green – which we would clear as a base for the guns. It was a shambles and I thought, This is not a good omen.

After a bit of a rest, we had to go back down the mountain and tramp across that bloody moor again. We were to lead the way for the rest of the battalion and tabbed back south in the direction of Goose Green and the neighbouring hamlet of Darwin. Both were on a peninsula, and the Argies had used their ample time to construct impressive defences. After tabbing for four or five hours, we neared Camilla Creek House – our start line for the battle – and Neame called up some artillery fire as a precaution to clear any Argies who might be lurking about. We were all deeply unimpressed when the shells landed a thousand yards *behind* us. There was much muttering about useless artillery, and we were lucky not to have been killed by our own side. After establishing that there were no Argies present, we moved in and were soon joined by Jones and his HQ staff. Even though we were presenting a concentrated target, we crammed into every nook and cranny of the old house and its outbuildings in a desperate bid to get warm. There were even paras curled up in the toilets, trying to thaw out and snatch some sleep. After a week in the open, it felt strange to be under a roof again.

Suddenly, we were all told to scatter and take up dispersed positions because our commanders feared that we might come under air attack. Then we learned the reason for their anxiety. Incredibly, the BBC had announced our plans to the whole world, including the Argies. You could not make it up. The bosses had been listening to the BBC World Service the previous night and had heard the newsreader announcing that the 2nd Battalion of the Parachute Regiment was poised to assault Darwin and Goose Green. So much for the element of surprise! Jones went apeshit and threatened to sue the BBC, Whitehall and the War Cabinet. Chris Keeble was all for abandoning the attack altogether. But Jones was keen to get stuck in, so he gambled – rightly, as it turned out – that the Argies would think the cock-up had been a ruse. After all, surely no country would be so monumentally bloody stupid as to broadcast details of an attack during a war!

As the battle drew closer, we were all hoping that we would perform to the best of our ability. We were apprehensive but not really afraid. Our biggest fear was not getting the job done right. We didn't know what we were getting into, but the officers assured us it would all be over by breakfast. Jones sent eight scouts to the north of the farmhouse, to check the approaches to Darwin. But they failed to spot the well-entrenched and well-camouflaged Argie machine-gun emplacements that were dug into the contours of Darwin Hill. Earlier SAS scouts had missed them, too. We would pay a heavy price for that.

At around 2.30 a.m. on 28 May, the Battle of Goose Green finally kicked off. A Company were the first to cross the start line, and they moved up to Burnside House, on the east side of the peninsula, where they were engaged by Argies. The paras killed two of the defenders and riddled the house with bullets. The enemy retreated, but when our guys went inside they were horrified to find three terrified British civilians. Fortunately, they were badly shaken but unhurt. Their house had more holes than a Swiss cheese, and they were lucky to be alive. This was another black mark against our intelligence, as we had been assured that no civvies were present.

The guns of the commandos' artillery opened up and shells from HMS *Arrow* came crashing in on Argie positions, too. Next, our mortars opened fire from about a mile behind us and gave the enemy a real pounding. A and B companies now moved towards Darwin, unknowingly heading straight for the concealed Argie machine guns and trenches. It was here that we suffered our first casualty, when Corporal Cork was hit in the stomach. He was later found dead, with Private Fletcher lying next to him, clutching a field dressing. Fletcher had been trying to administer first aid when he too had been shot dead.

Officially, my company – D Company – were the reserves. I was thinking, OK, we're in reserve, so we might not have to do a lot here. I was put straight on that pretty quick. We were dropped into it right from the start, and were then in the shit all the time. By the end of the war, we had lost more men than any other company in 2 Para.

A firefight started up right in front of us and we hit the deck. All of a sudden, it was like hell on earth. Machine-gun fire was coming at us from all angles and it was pretty accurate, too. The Argies were also firing shamooli flares straight at us instead of into the air to illuminate our positions. There were different-coloured tracers cutting through the darkness – their tracers, our tracers. Green, white and red. It was strangely beautiful, but as we clawed into the ground we had little time to admire the view. Machine guns, mortars and rifles added to the chaos. I didn't know who was firing at who. No fucking idea. I tried to get my bearings. 'Where's the gunfire coming from? Where are our boys? Where are the Argies?' Shouts, screams and explosions contributed to the bedlam. Then I heard an even stranger noise, one that I had never experienced in training. 'What the hell was that?' I shouted as I spun around. Then I saw a terrible sight silhouetted against the burning farm buildings – wild horses were running around in the flames and smoke, rearing up in distress at the madness of men.

At first, I was shit scared, but then the adrenalin kicked in. For the first time in a week, I was not cold. The fighting spirit took over and my fear vanished. I was a fighting machine and ready to go. In the middle of this maelstrom, I achieved an amazing clarity. A series of thoughts ran through my mind: What are our objectives? Trust in your training. Remember the teamwork. Keep your buddies going. Do the fucking job. It's pure chance whether you are injured or killed in war. Survival is all down to pot luck. If it's meant for you, you'll get it.

This was the first time we had come under fire. I knew that it was a case of kill or be killed. I had complete faith in my training, and sure enough it kicked in straight away. You have to trust that it will work and trust the comrades who are standing beside you. The key in battle is to keep the momentum going, keep moving forward. It was dark, pure chaos, and we didn't know where the Argie positions were until we were right on top of them. Tracers were zinging all over the place and machine-gun bullets whipped through the air. Mortars, grenades and anti-tank weapons were exploding. White phosphorus was going off, providing bursts of dazzling illumination. Men were screaming in terror and pain. We got into the enemy trenches. The air was thick with smoke and the smell of burning gorse mingled with the pungent odour of blood and punctured guts. We stumbled over dead Argies and then came across their terrified comrades. Some of them were jabbering away, crying and waving their hands in the air. Others were writhing and squealing in agony as searing-hot phosphorus burned and burrowed its way through their flesh. You know that your mates are being killed and injured too, and all you can think is: 'Please God, get me through this battle.' But your officer keeps yelling, 'Move! Move! Move!' and you keep moving forward.

By now, the shit was really hitting the fan. We had reached a place called Coronation Ridge and were pinned down by a machine-gun nest. Two English guys, Lance Corporal Gary 'Gaz' Bingley and his number two, Private Barry 'Baz' Grayling, went forward to try to take the position with one of the platoon's three machine guns. They charged towards the Argies, with Bingley firing from the hip. He killed two Argies but was hit in the head by the last shots they managed to loose off. Grayling's life was probably saved by his water bottle, which was hit directly by an enemy bullet.

There was no time to think. We needed that Gimpy, which was now lying on the ground, just feet from the Argie trench. The firepower was crucial for us – without the gun, we were screwed. I had no thoughts about personal safety or how to go about it. It was a case of '*Fuck it!* Get out there Tony and get that fucking gun.' *Whoosh*, I was up, away and sprinting the fifteen yards or so to Bingley and Grayling. The firefight was raging all around me. When I reached them, I knew immediately that Bingley was dead. It was pitch dark, so I couldn't see any injuries, but I grabbed his arm and it was heavy and limp. Lifeless. But at that moment it didn't really register with me that a guy I'd seen every day was dead, gone. You can't allow yourself to dwell on it. I was more concerned that we were a man down. And he was a section leader, so he had a key role to play. It was a numbers game. Our power had just been reduced by one.

I got angry with Grayling because he wouldn't move. We were totally exposed and bullets were whizzing past our ears. We needed to get the fuck out of there. *Now.* But Grayling thought he had been shot. He hadn't been, thanks to his lucky water bottle. I grabbed him and shouted, 'You're OK, you're OK. Let's go. Come on. Let's get back.' In the end, I had to haul him and the gun back to our position. While I was doing that, the others advanced and gave the surviving Argies in the trench a horrible death by chucking in a phosphorous grenade.

Once we'd regrouped, the advance began again. Using what cover we could find – any little dip in the ground, up the side of hollows – we leapfrogged our way forward. At one point, we stopped to turn our machine guns on some Argies who were running along the beach behind us. Amid the chaos, we had to keep our structure and discipline and not go off on tangents or lose our way. We all knew our objectives. Then, all of a sudden, more well-concealed Argies opened up on us. *Holy shit!* We scrambled back up the valley but were painfully exposed to a new and deadly danger – snipers. As we frantically scraped a few precious inches into the ground, one of our lads, Tam Mechan, took a bullet which went right through the front of his helmet and out the back. Poor Tam. He was supposed to have been out of the army, but he had been talked into doing another six months.

Wayne 'Taff' Rees was on the Gimpy, pouring fire at the Argies, and eventually the anti-tank guys came up and blasted the positions where we thought the snipers were hiding. It must have been hell for them, but it was still dangerous for us, too. If a bullet had your name on it, only God or Lady Luck could help – as my good mate Dave Parr found out. He went down like a pile of bricks when he was struck in the belly by an Argie bullet. As Dave lay groaning on the ground, a medic dashed to his assistance but was puzzled by the lack of blood. When he cut away Dave's clothing, he made an amazing discovery – the bullet was lying in his belly button. It had hit his webbing and travelled along his belt. The force of the impact had left Dave winded and badly bruised, but he had lived to fight another day.

I was one of the older blokes in the platoon, even though I was only twenty. Amazingly, we had some seventeen-year-olds with us. They were too young to be sent to the streets of Northern Ireland, they couldn't even vote or drink legally, but they were old enough to get their bollocks blown off in the South Atlantic. We were all just young laddies, but we were quite mature for our age, especially compared to the Argies. As we advanced, we came across trenches and positions they had abandoned. We found loads of toy cars and comic books, letters from home and photos of loved ones. It was sad. Generally, their trenches were a mess. Pink toilet paper and shit lay everywhere, rubbish was strewn about and the dugouts were poorly constructed. But the Argies were still not to be underestimated. Anyone pointing a gun at you has to be respected. I kept telling myself, 'Do not feel sorry for these bastards. Do not feel sorry for them.' We couldn't afford to have any sympathy for them. Instead, we rolled forward and killed everything in our path.

Breakfast time came and went. It was daylight now and we were still fighting. I started to think that this was not going to plan. Our artillery support was weakened when the gun on HMS *Arrow* jammed. Then our air support was hampered when bad weather stopped the Harriers from taking off. Then the artillery ran short of ammunition. Our mortars had had it, too. This was not looking good. We were supposed to advance under covering fire. To make matters worse, the Argies were putting up much stiffer resistance than we'd expected and were still firing heavily on us. A and B companies were bogged down and were under withering fire from a network of eleven mutually supporting trenches near Darwin Hill. It was a stalemate.

Then the news came over the comms that 'Sunray' was down. 'Sunray' was Colonel H Jones's call sign, and the message could mean only one thing: our commanding officer had been killed in action. We learned later that he had led a suicidal charge against one of those machine-gun posts on Darwin Hill.

It was a stunning blow. But it was crazy, too. Jones had not only got himself killed but had led our popular adjutant, Captain Dave Wood, and a radio operator to their deaths. Shortly after their failed assault, the enemy trenches were taken out with anti-tank rockets and the surviving Argies on the hill surrendered. My view is that Jones should never have been in that position in the first place. He was in the Falklands to lead the whole of 2 Para, not a small assault force. He was gung-ho and brave but irresponsible. For that reason, it rankled with me that he was later awarded a posthumous Victoria Cross.

Meanwhile, other machine-gun posts continued to give us real trouble. We had to inch forward and get as close as we could before lobbing in grenades. That was the most effective way of dealing with them. Once the grenades had gone in, we would find a lot of dead Argies, and for a millisecond you couldn't help but pity them. In the trenches there would be rifles with pictures of the Virgin Mary and the baby Jesus pasted on the butts, and rosary beads twined around machine guns. At one point, I thought: They're Catholics, like me. Young laddies, like me. We had been praying to the same God, but it hadn't done them much good. But then my training kicked in again. I knew that if I was to survive, if we were to win, I could not afford to feel sorry for them. It was time to move on and kill or be killed. That was all there was to it.

Our next target – Boca House – was taken after a fierce gun battle that was settled for good when our anti-tank guys fired Milan missiles into the Argie positions. These weapons were intended to punch their way through armour plating, but their improvised use by 2 Para against machine-gun nests and Argie trenches played a big part in our success. The surviving defenders were quick to surrender and a lot of prisoners were taken.

As we went through the Argie positions, we saw some truly gruesome sights. Heads had been blasted off and faces were hideously contorted with ghastly gaping holes. Some of them had wide-open eyes, as if caught by surprise. One guy was still alive but had no arms. We found the two limbs yards away from him, on either side of the trench. It was amazing how quickly we became used to such macabre scenes. Dead Argies were slumped over their machine guns. We would hoist them up, fling them aside and then check to see if any of their kit might be of some use to us. Their boots were certainly much better than ours, so a lot of guys literally helped themselves to dead men's shoes. It was a battle rite that had gone on for centuries, and now we were perpetuating it.

Gunshot wounds were the most common cause of death. A corpse might look relatively unscathed from the front, with just a small round patch of blood marking the entry point of a bullet. But when we turned the body over, the exit wound would be huge and messy, with blood and gunge spread everywhere. A hit in the middle of the chest would leave blood and bits splattered all over the guy's back, shoulders, arms and even down to his legs. And the victims always seemed to be young guys – fresh-faced, but dirty, unkempt and pathetic. I wondered why they didn't wash. They'd had plenty of time to dig-in and get organised before we arrived. They should have had a plentiful supply of water for drinking and bathing, and time to wash and shave, so there was no need to get shitty and smelly. But I couldn't dwell on the cruel fate of these guys. It was a morale thing. You couldn't afford to be mentally brought down, because you wouldn't be at your best if you let it get to you. You just had to think, Fuck you, you were shooting at me, and move on.

We advanced on the left flank, alongside a beach, which we soon learned had been mined by the Argies. My mate Taff Rees saw an explosion to his left and one of our guys blown twenty feet into the air. But after he'd come back down to earth, the guy just stood up, dusted himself down, picked up his rifle, and charged on. Taff told me later, 'The Argies must have thought we were fucking supermen!' Luckily for us, the Argies had laid their mines too deep, so most of the explosion was absorbed by the peaty ground. Otherwise, the guy would never have survived.

We were heading towards an airfield that was squeezed between well-entrenched enemy positions at Goose Green. Then, out of nowhere, an Argentinian Pucara zoomed overhead with its cannons blazing. We hunkered down and started returning fire with our semi-automatics, machine guns, whatever we had to hand. Incredibly, smoke started to appear from the plane and it plunged into the ground. It was like something out of the movies. A huge cheer went up. It was better than a Celtic goal at Ibrox.

We moved forward, but before long we were bogged down again. We were taking fire from a heavily fortified schoolhouse and its surrounding trenches, and there was no doubt that these Argies were lethally accurate. I heard a cry and saw that Steve Dixon, a good mate of mine, had been shot. I ran over to him but the colour was already draining from his face and he was turning a bluish grey. His breathing was shallow. He was done in. I didn't want to see this, but I was wide-eyed. Every detail of Steve's last moments was seared into my consciousness. The young Essex boy who had been my mate all through training sighed his last word: 'Mum.' Then a single tear rolled down his face. It was a devastating moment and that vivid image has stayed with me ever since.

It affects you deeply when you lose a lad from your own platoon. There are only thirty of you, and you live in each other's pockets day in, day out, so you know each other intimately. It's like losing a member of your family, a loved one.

Finally, a white flag appeared at the schoolhouse and three lads from 12 Platoon – led by platoon commander Jim Barry – went to take the surrender. But as they approached the building the Argies opened up on them and shot them dead. That was it for us. Watching our guys being mown down in that manner was the last straw. It was gutless, pitiless and disgusting in the extreme. When it happened, we all looked on in disbelief, then jumped up as one and unloaded on the place. A rocket and a couple of phosphorous grenades soon had the schoolhouse ablaze. Even if we'd run out of ammunition, we would have marched down there and kicked the shit out of them. Guys were going nuts, shouting, screaming, 'You dirty spic bastards! Filthy dagos! Greasy wop bastards!' That was the one and only time I heard any hardcore racism during the whole conflict. By the time we'd finished, the building had been obliterated and dozens of Argies had been killed. Not one of them was left to surrender this time.

Rocky and I went on towards the airfield and found some deserted Argie trenches. They were well constructed and were partly roofed over. We decided to hunker down and get a brew on. The battle had been raging all night, so a cup of tea was well overdue. We got the stove lit but then heard an aircraft coming over and a load of firing. We looked at each other and said, 'Fuck it!' We reckoned there were more than enough guys out there to deal with it. Our priority was to get this brew done, and we were enjoying a well-deserved cuppa when a bunch of guys came in, all geared up. 'Did you see that?' they asked. 'They dropped fucking napalm on us.' Rocky and I had missed the whole thing – the first time the British Army had ever suffered a napalm attack.

Looking around the schoolhouse, there were body parts everywhere. Some lumps of charred flesh were barely recognisable as ever having been human beings, but we dealt with it in the usual squaddie way – with sick humour. You would walk past a dead body and think, He wasn't sitting like that before. Some of our guys were having their photographs taken with the corpses, putting their arms around them and placing them in compromising positions. Sometimes the black humour would go even further. One of the mortar sergeants, Pip Hall, let out a yelp when he opened his rucksack and half a human leg fell out. I guess war affects people in crazy ways.

While we were sorting out the bodies, we were told that Chris Keeble had used a couple of Argie prisoners to deliver an ultimatum to their commanders: surrender or face bombardment. Then we learned that we had been assigned to head into Goose Green and accept the surrender. Almost as soon as we'd done that, the prisoners started to drift in – and there were hundreds of the bastards. There must have been between 1200 and 1500 of them. We could not believe it. 2 Para was a battalion of just 500 men. Usually, the British Army likes to fight with a ratio of three of us to one of the enemy, but in this instance the ratio had been flipped in the Argies' favour. Sheer guts and bloody determination had won the day for us. The fourteen-hour battle had cost the British a total of seventeen killed and sixty-four wounded, with the majority from 2 Para. Eight of those killed and two of the wounded were from D Company. Around fifty Argentinians had been killed and one hundred and twenty wounded.

We herded the prisoners into a huge sheep shed, with 'POW' written on the roof in huge letters to save it from being attacked. During the fighting, we had come across a lot of Argie conscripts, but a significant number of these prisoners were regular army and air force personnel. They were generally quite submissive. In fact, they were pathetic. A lot of them seemed undernourished – despite the plentiful food stockpiles that we found – and they were plainly glad it was all over. I later learned that they had endured tough treatment at the hands of their own officers. But we didn't know that at the time. Nor did we care. Once the war was over, many of them would say that they were looked after better by us than by their own.

One prisoner stood out from the crowd, mainly because he was wearing a maroon beret. I didn't know whether he was an officer or a special ops guy, but he certainly looked a cut above the rest. He had this air of superiority about him. Unlike the others, he wasn't sheepish or weak, scuffing the dirt with his boots. He was standing there above it all, in his shit-hot beret. A red mist of rage descended on me and I thought, Fuck him. Arrogant bastard. Tossers like him started this whole thing. And why has he still got his hat on when nobody else has? It pissed me right off. I walked up to him and knocked the beret off his head. Then, as he looked at me with some defiance, I smashed my rifle butt into his face. He dropped to his knees and I walked off with his beret. *Fuck him.* I fingered the beret and found a single round sewn inside – presumably a last round that he had intended to use on himself rather than surrender. But then he must have bottled out when the time had come.

Of course, if I'd been caught mistreating a prisoner, I would have been in the shit. But I'd had more than enough of the Argies by then, given how many men we'd lost. I almost wanted one of them to step out of line. As far as I was concerned, if there was any shit, I had no qualms about shooting the bastards. My attitude was: you fuck around and I'll shoot you. I wouldn't have blinked an eyelid. I was a fuming cauldron of rage.

Slowly, locals started to emerge from the church and village hall. They were so grateful for us being there. We were heroes to them and we felt like liberators. They showered us with goodies and produced welcome bottles of vodka and whisky. It was great to be a part of it all. When we saw them, and discovered that they were just like us Brits, not like Argies at all, we thought, Yes, this is right – what we've done here. Their houses had been wrecked by the occupiers, who seemed to have used every room as a toilet. The villagers couldn't do enough for us. I was thrilled when I was introduced to one fella who was a radio ham and he let me send a message back to my mum and dad, telling them that I was OK. The battle had been on 28 May – Mum's birthday.

It was a great victory, especially as it was achieved without full artillery or air support against superior numbers who were well dug-in. But we had paid a heavy price for Goose Green. We organised a mass burial for the dead at Ajax Bay, with Padre Cooper doing his bit. It was grim. Soldiers walked into the big grave with body bags, laid them down and walked off, so the next guys could come along and do the same. A mass grave? In 1982? It seemed unreal. And horrendous.

After the funeral, I saw Major Keeble walking past. I approached him and asked, 'Is that it for us then, sir?'

He looked at me and considered his answer carefully before replying, 'You've done well.'

It was a telling, worrying response. My heart sank. I thought we had done our bit by taking Goose Green. I thought we would dig in and let others take over from here. But no – we were to fight another battle. The worst was yet to come.

CHAPTER 4

FIX BAYONETS!

When the fighting stopped at Goose Green, we were all basically in a state of shock. Guys were wandering around with their eyes wide open and glazed expressions – like stunned mullets. Our bodies were beginning to readjust to some kind of normality as the adrenalin ebbed from us. Overwhelming fatigue also began to set in. We had been repeatedly subjected to near-death stress for thirty-six hours – the sort of stress that most people encounter only once or twice, if ever, in their lives. We had cheated death again and again, but we had done so in a state of extreme and heightened tension. It was like narrowly avoiding a head-on collision every few minutes over the course of a day and a half. Unknown to us, that stress would take its toll in later years. But, for now, we were elated. We had won a brilliant victory against the odds and we were still alive. We had survived while seventeen of our comrades had died and many more had been wounded.

Thoughts of the horrors we had seen kept flooding back, however, and I could not get the image of Steve Dixon's last moments out of my mind. Other flashbacks of men dying terrible and agonising deaths stormed through my consciousness, too. It had not been like the movies, where people slipped away quietly while murmuring a few poignant last words to their mates as they died in their arms. And we were still surrounded by horrific sights as we set about tidying up the battlefield. For three or four days after the shooting stopped, we would continue to find Argentinian dead and wounded. The rows of bodies dumped at the airfield grew longer and longer.

Our medics were under real pressure, with lots of serious cases and many men near death. Some of them wanted to treat our lads first, which I thought was fair enough, but the officers insisted that the Argentinian wounded, many of whom had gangrene setting in, should not be neglected.

Padre Cooper set about burying the Argentinian dead without much help from the Argie chaplains – only one out of the three or four offered to help. The Argie officers didn't seem to take much interest in their men, either. I thought it was strange that we had found plentiful supplies of food yet so many of the young Argies looked undernourished and were grateful for the grub we gave them. Some had either sandshoes or wellington boots on their feet – totally unsuited for the terrain and climate. But others – maybe regulars or special forces – seemed well fed and kitted out.

We could not get over the huge number of prisoners and the vast piles of rifles and kit we had captured – including leaky napalm canisters. We kept ourselves busy and set up defensive positions in case of an Argie counter-attack. Some of the Argies volunteered to help tidy up, which came as a relief as we were very worried about booby-traps and trip-wires. Suddenly, as a group of them were clearing a pile of ammunition, there was a terrific explosion and one of the Argies had his legs and arms blown off. The stumps were horrifically burned around the exposed bone.

After our memorial service – taken by Chris Keeble, who seemed a natural in the pulpit – we enjoyed some celebrations with the islanders. As they died down, I began to reflect on the battle and came to the conclusion that we had been bloody lucky. The Argies had put up stiff resistance and it seemed to me that we had won despite a series of massive cock-ups. It had all gone wrong right from the start – our unexpected amphibious landing had been a sign of things to come. The loss of the Chinooks on board the *Atlantic*

Conveyor, the trench foot and frostbite casualties, the BBC broadcasting our plans, HMS *Arrow*'s one and only gun jamming, poor weather grounding the Harriers, our failure to use the light armoured cars that had been available, Colonel Jones getting himself and Dave Wood killed, our poor artillery and mortar support and faulty intelligence – it all pointed to an army that was overstretched and under-resourced. But that just rekindled my pride in being a member of 2 Para. We had triumphed in spite of all the fuck-ups.

Nevertheless, I didn't fancy going into battle again. That brief conversation with Chris Keeble – when he had let me know we had more work to do – had really got me thinking. It was like your second parachute jump. You were not frightened during the first one, but once you knew what to expect, the second one scared the shit out of you. I knew I had been lucky at Goose Green, and I did not want to stretch that luck too far. But I had no say in the matter, of course. A few days later, we were on the move again.

At least this time we went by chopper, thank God. It was good to be in the RAF's one and only surviving Chinook. We felt like paras again. It was 2 June when the chopper touched down near a deserted Argie outpost on a barren hillside overlooking a slate-grey cove. It was freezing, with the odd flake of snow blowing through, but we managed to find some cover in the shape of some huge sheep-shearing sheds. The place was called Fitzroy, and below us was Bluff Cove. I checked the map I had pinched after Colonel Jones's briefing and discovered that the whole area was called Port Pleasant. As our three-foot-deep trenches quickly became waterlogged, I did not appreciate the cartographer's sense of humour. There was nothing pleasant about this place or the freezing winds that were whipping in from Antarctica.

I believe the plan was for us to get a bit of rest. By now, a whole brigade of five thousand men had arrived. The previous week, there had been only us and two companies of marines, along with the SAS and SBS squads. But the *QEII* had finally turned up with the Scots Guards, the Welsh Guards and the Gurkhas. 3 Para were on the islands, too. The bosses were in the process of planning the final assault on Port Stanley, which would involve seizing the six or seven hills which lay in front of it, and they now had the men and the firepower to do it.

Sitting in those bloody trenches was every bit as miserable as the days we spent on Sussex Mountain, and more men were already going down with frostbite. But at least we had the sheep-shearing sheds, where we could have a wash and get warm. While we were digging in, two ships slipped into the bay below. First was the *Sir Tristram*, followed the next day by the *Sir Galahad*. Both were packed with more troops and ammunition. They were anchored close to each other, fifty yards offshore – two tempting, undefended targets sitting side by side. But for some strange reason the troops were kept aboard as the logistics were taken off. Rapier air defences were being erected, but it was obvious that in the meantime these guys were sitting ducks. We kept asking, 'Why don't they get those guys ashore?' It seemed mental. The *Sir Galahad* had already had two miraculous escapes. It was one of the ships that we had seen attacked in San Carlos Bay. Three days after it had landed 350 marines, Argentinian Skyhawks had swooped down and dropped a thousand-pound bomb on it. Luckily, it had failed to detonate and had been safely defused. In the second attack, the ship had been strafed by enemy fighters. Unknown to us, the Argies now had an observation post on a distant hill, and they once again had the *Sir Galahad* in their sights.

We were still muttering about the crazy situation down in the bay when we moved into one of the sheep-shearing sheds. It was full of wooden pens and we could squeeze four guys into each one, which allowed us to have a wee kip and chill out. Before long, the shed was full of paras. That was mad too. The Argies could have wiped us all out with a single missile.

After six days in there, with the shock of Goose Green becoming a memory, the old problems started returning. Guys were fed up and started moaning. We were becoming fractious, too, and tempers were frayed. In one of the pens, a negligent discharge led to a guy being shot in the stomach. We were all on edge, and more and more of us had problems with our feet because of the perpetual damp and our crappy boots. One day, around two o'clock in the afternoon, I was working on my feet when I suddenly heard Argie planes screaming overhead. There was a tremendous roar of machine guns and explosions. The shit was really hitting the fan out there. We had to disperse out of that shed and quick. I ran outside in my bare feet and dived into a trench. Down below, we could see that the *Sir Galahad*'s luck had finally run out. It was being attacked by five Argentinian Skyhawks and thick black smoke was already billowing out of the vessel as fierce fires engulfed its stern. At first, we thought everyone on board must have bought it. But then we saw guys jumping over the side and into the freezing water – which had burning oil floating on the surface. Orange life-rafts were being chucked over the side, too. Guys were burning down there, trapped and screaming in terror and agony as the fire spread. Of course, I knew it was serious, but I didn't know that I was witnessing Britain's biggest disaster of the whole war. One of my mates gave me a piggy back to the shed and I frantically pulled on my boots before running down to the beach with the rest of the lads. Once again, the adrenalin kicked in and we covered a long distance in a short space of time. When we arrived, bullets were whistling and zipping past us as the ammunition stores aboard the *Sir Galahad* blew up. From down on the beach, it was clear that the *Sir Tristram* had also been hit by the Argie attack squadron.

It was a horrendous scene, but amid the chaos there was some amazing bravery. Men dashed into smoke-filled corridors to rescue comrades trapped by the spreading flames. A Wessex helicopter enveloped in smoke lowered a winchman in his orange survival suit to pluck survivors from the inferno. Then came the most astonishing sight of all. The wind had got up and was starting to blow some of the life-rafts back towards the burning ship. Four of them, packed with badly injured casualties, were drifting helplessly towards the still-exploding *Sir Galahad*. We watched in horror from the shore, unable to do anything to save them. Then one Wessex, followed by another, and another, and another came down and hovered over the life-rafts, blowing them away from the danger and into the shore and safety. They were like mother hens protecting their chicks. It was incredible to see.

We pulled the life-rafts up and on to the shore, and found the casualties in a shocking state. They were mainly Welsh Guards, and many were screaming in excruciating pain from their burns. In some cases, their clothes had melted on to their scorched bodies. The sights and the smells were dreadful –

totally unforgettable. Cutting through the smell of cordite and phosphorus, the terrible stench of burning flesh clung to the inside of our nostrils. We tried to lift the most badly burned on to stretchers as carefully as we could, but every movement had them crying out for their mothers. Others stumbled up the beach in complete shock, holding out arms with ribbons of skin trailing down from the bubbling flesh. We rushed the stretcher cases up to the regimental aid post as fast as we could and tried to calm them: 'Don't worry, mate. You'll be fine. You're OK. Our medics will soon fix you up.' I knew I was lying through my teeth, but reassuring words were all we had. I had seen dead and wounded at Goose Green, but they were blast injuries and gunshot wounds. We knew all about that type of injury. We had all attended classes during the voyage and learned about entry and exit wounds. But we really weren't prepared for what we were seeing and smelling down on that beach. It was truly horrific. The smell was so distinctive. Years later, I was shocked to smell it once again. I was driving down the M6 and they were burning all the animals that had been culled during the foot and mouth epidemic. The smell wafted into the car and with it came vivid memories of Fitzroy.

Of course, we felt deeply sorry for the *Sir Galahad* guys, but we were relieved it had not been us on the receiving end of Galtieri's five-hundred-pound bombs. We were closely bonded in 2 Para and, as bad as it was, it did not feel quite as bad as if it had been our guys in the inferno. We felt ever so slightly detached from the situation. They weren't *our* blokes, *our* team, *our* para regiment. As callous as that sounds, it probably helped us to be more effective and functional during the rescue operation.

Amid the mayhem, groups of Chinese seafarers from Hong Kong who worked for the Royal Fleet Auxiliary appeared. Some of them were burned black and were covered in tar. Their hair had been burned off and their swollen eyes were closed. They were helpless. When one of our guys grabbed one of them by the arm, all the skin came off like a sleeve. Most of them seemed stunned and bewildered. And they looked strangely out of place in that freezing and barren landscape.

Fifty-six men died and over a hundred and fifty were wounded in the attacks on the two ships at Fitzroy. Among the wounded was Welsh Guardsman Simon Weston, who suffered 49 per cent burns to his body but still went on to become a champion of ex-servicemen. Those who weren't seriously wounded were taken up to the sheds for a cup of tea, but eventually we started to get a bit angry with them. They started giving away their kit and saying things like, 'Ah well, lads, that's our war over. They'll be sending us home soon. We'll leave it in your capable hands.'

I was furious. We'd been through the mill, too. I thought, You sheep-shagging crap-hat bastards. You haven't done anything yet.

Later, when I learned about the balls-up that had left them exposed to the enemy, I had a lot more sympathy for them. It was yet another costly mistake by the British Army. I was angered by the waste and loss of life caused by sheer stupidity, bumbling and unnecessary delays. The captain of the ship had told the Welsh Guards to get off; a furious marine major had told them to get off. They knew they were far too exposed anchored there in Fitzroy. But the Welsh Guards officers disagreed and the result was that some blokes never got off that ship. Eventually the burned-out hulk of the *Sir Galahad* was towed out to sea and sunk. The site was declared an official war grave.

Little did we know that it could have been even worse. The Argentinian Air Force had sent in a second wave of fighter bombers, but they had been intercepted by RAF Harriers and three Argie pilots had been killed in the engagement.

With the Welsh Guards effectively out of the picture, we knew that we would soon be back on the front line. Fortunately, although Fitzroy had been a heavy blow, it had not crushed our morale. The Argie commander had been told that hundreds had been killed in the raid and he had expected our fighting spirit to collapse. The exact opposite was the case.

Our attitude was: 'Let's get stuck in. We have the animal cornered, so let's finish it off.' Everyone was confident that we were the aggressors now, not the Argies. We had taken the fight to the Argies at Goose Green and they hadn't liked it. We had a new commander, too: Lieutenant Colonel David Chaundler had been chosen to replace H Jones. He had parachuted into the sea to join us, leading one of the battalion wits to speculate that he might have been the man from the Milk Tray adverts.

Barely thirty-six hours after the carnage at Fitzroy, we were on the move again. Our task was to take Wireless Ridge, with the assault scheduled for the night of 10 June. It was the last great Argentinian stronghold before Port Stanley, with excellent natural defences. Before getting to the Argie positions, we would have to weave our way through a series of hollows, rocky ledges, undulations, outcrops and, of course, minefields. We were attacking from the north, with those of us in D Company on one flank, alongside A and B companies, and the SAS coming in from the other side. A telegraph line marked our first stop line. The enemy had an entire regiment up there waiting for us, so the idea was to capture one objective at a time and concentrate our firepower on it before moving on.

Our assault was part of a massive offensive designed to smash Argentinian resolve. Mount Tumbledown and

Wireless Ridge overlooked each other, allowing the Argies to set up cross-fire, so it was essential to attack both simultaneously. The Scots Guards were handed the task of going in on Tumbledown. The Argie stronghold on neighbouring Mount Longdon was already under attack from 3 Para, 45 Commando was attacking another mountain strongpoint – Twin Sisters – and troops from 42 Commando were hitting Mount Harriet. The Argies were certainly going to be kept busy.

It all seemed very straightforward, and the preparations at least took our minds off the terrible scenes we had witnessed at Fitzroy. Before we were choppered into position at the foot of Mount Kent, the cooks knocked up a last supper. Everyone knows an army marches on its stomach, and what could be nicer than a morale-boosting hot meal? We had been on our standard rations for over a week now, and many of the guys were suffering from constipation. The cooks erected a sign welcoming us to 'Fitzroy café' with the warning: 'If you like the service, tell your friends. If you don't, hand your food back and draw a 24-hr ration pack.' A sheep had been slaughtered and the resulting mutton stew was delicious. We joked that maybe the Falklands and their sheep were worth fighting for after all. It was a welcome change from our boring ration packs.

The choppers then took us the five miles to Mount Kent

and we started another grim night-time march to our starting point. As we tabbed in single file, once again stumbling over tussocks of grass and staggering through peat bogs, we came under sudden and unexpected attack ... from diarrhoea. The sheep was exacting powerful revenge on us, and man after man fell out to drop his trousers and answer an urgent call of nature. This was not part of the plan – and neither was the subsequent twenty-four-hour delay in our attack. As usual, the best-laid plans of mice and men had gone agley.

It was snowing, and we dug in to the lee of the hill, out of sight of the Argies, to try to keep warm as we waited to go in. As we shivered and froze in sub-zero temperatures, we cursed the Scots Guards for not being ready and delaying the attack. But they had actually done us a favour. Chaundler used the delay to concentrate more artillery firepower for the forth-coming battle. He had learned from Goose Green, where we had gambled on a surprise attack with only limited artillery support. The Argies now knew we were coming, but they didn't know when and they didn't know from which direc-tion. So the planned massive barrage would not rob us of the element of surprise. We were freezing but safe in our dug-outs. The Argies couldn't shell us, but if we exposed ourselves we were still vulnerable. One of our guys went to have a crap. He arrived at a flat area at the foot of the hill and the next thing he knew mortars were raining down on him. He had his trousers around his ankles and we were falling about laughing as he tried to pull them up while running back. We were still laughing when he dived into the scrape. But that stopped when he pulled a massive lump of shrapnel from his webbing. He had been inches from death – a very lucky boy.

The build-up to Wireless Ridge seemed to go on for ever. We had various advance points from where we would attack the ridge, but it was pitch black and we couldn't really make out any features of the landscape, aside from the large black mass of the ridge itself. It was too cold to sleep, so we had a second night without any shut-eye. We had also run out of rations, so we had to rely on what we had stuffed into our kits.

In the morning, we got our first proper sight of the ridge and realised that it was a perfect defensive position. There were hundreds of massive granite shards, like axe heads, that looked like they had been dropped into the earth sequentially from a great height. The Argies could hide behind these bulletproof 'walls' and pop away at us.

Before we launched our attack, the promised massive barrage went over. It was fantastic stuff. The Argies were pounded for hours. Chaundler was adamant that we would never enter battle without massive bombing and air support. As uplifting as the barrage was for us, it must have been soul destroying for the Argies. It was a constant menace to them and we wondered how any of them could possibly survive it.

Shells would whistle over our heads, then there would be a dull thud and the sky would light up in the distance with a terrific explosion. It went on and on. Our artillery and mortars kept the enemy's heads well down. We had plenty of anti-tank Milan missiles, too, which had served us well at Goose Green. And for the first time we also had Scimitar light tanks and Scorpion armoured cars. They put down a load of heavy fire and used tracers to light up the enemy positions. All of this was important because the Argies' heavy machine guns could outrange us, and they had been lethal at Goose Green. It was also a big boost to our morale.

We had hoped that D Company would be kept in reserve because of our earlier losses, but it was not to be. It turned out later that Chaundler had been informed that we had avoided the worst of the fighting at Goose Green, which was why he deployed us at Wireless Ridge! As we marched to the start line in extended order, I thought, This is crazy. It's like the First World War. We're all going to get mown down by machine guns. My stomach tightened and I repeated the prayer that I had said at Goose Green: 'Please God, get me through this battle. Just get me through this.' My level of fear had increased and the prayer grew more fervent each time I mouthed the words. I knew what to expect, I did not want to die and above all I did not want to die an agonising death on a freezing-cold, dark hillside in the middle of nowhere. All of these thoughts ran through my head, just as they must have run through the minds of the lads in the trenches before the whistle was blown and the order was given to go over the top.

The guns finally fell silent and out of the gloom came a dreaded order. Again, it would have been familiar to the Tommies in 1914: 'Fix bayonets, lads! Fix bayonets!' It was a stomach-churning moment. Oh fuck, here we go, I thought. The British Army hadn't gone in with bayonets since the Second World War. Then an even more awful instruction: 'No prisoners, lads. No prisoners.' Now we were about to run into this black abyss, not really knowing where the enemy was, not knowing the gradients or the whereabouts of their lines. It was madness.

Fucking hell, I thought. This is gonna be nasty!

We simply did not have the resources to take prisoners in the heat of battle. We were fighting in the pitch dark, and securing one prisoner could occupy two or three men whom we could not afford to lose. We respected prisoners taken after the battle, but they had little chance during the fighting itself. And we felt that they had little cause for complaint. After all, they had started the war and they had not shown much respect for the white flag when they had shot those three lads at the schoolhouse. What goes around comes around. This battle was all about momentum – keeping going and getting on with it.

This was it. 'Let's get on with it. Let's do it. Remember your training. Keep going. Keep going.' We launched our assault and scrambled forward through the peat bogs and what we later learned was a minefield. But when we reached the first positions, there was nobody there. The trenches had been abandoned. Fucking great, I thought. They've bolted. The sight of fleeing troops was always a downer for their comrades behind them, and these guys must have fled through their own lines.

We reorganised ourselves in the Argie defences but immediately came under shellfire from their artillery on Tumbledown, which had yet to be cleared by the Scots Guards. We turned left after that and started out along the ridge. That is where we met them face to face. All of a sudden it was like a scene from *Star Wars*, with tracer rounds flying everywhere. These guys were well armed, well disciplined and highly motivated. They had good positions and we had a helluva fight on our hands.

The battle ebbed and flowed as we came up against a series of well-entrenched machine-gun nests. During one attack, we called up artillery support with disastrous consequences. The artillery was supposed to soften up the Argie positions but instead five shells came crashing down almost on top of us. We realised the screw-up and someone started screaming down the radio: 'Check fire! Check fire!' But it was too late. Five more rounds were already in the air and coming straight towards us. I saw a shell hole in the ground and thought, What are the chances of two landing in exactly the same spot? So I dived in the hole, which was already half full of water, and cursed those stupid bastards in the artillery. I would remain soaked and freezing for the rest of the battle, just like the growing number of us who had plunged waist deep into peat bogs. But I had got off lightly. When I scrambled out of the hole, some of the guys were bending over a body, look-ing for any sign of life. My stomach sank when I saw it was Dave Parr, my mate from Lincolnshire who had had such a narrow escape at Goose Green when a bullet had lodged in his webbing. After a few days with the medics, he had hitched a ride on a helicopter and rejoined us at Fitzroy. No one had ordered him to do that. He had volunteered to be with his mates in 2 Para. Now he was dead – killed by his own side, a victim of so-called 'friendly fire'. Our young officer was going mental at the artillery guys, saying he would string them up. And I was especially devastated by Dave's death. After all, we had bunked together in the barracks at Aldershot. But we had to keep moving and leave him behind. His luck had run out.

Before long, we were fighting our way along the ridge. We bunged a grenade into an Argie position and made sure none of its occupants would give us any more trouble. Sometimes the Argies fought to the bitter end and sometimes young con-scripts just pulled their sleeping bags over their heads in the hope that it would all go away. But we could not take any chances with any of them. We had just cleared the trench when a terrified young Argie suddenly stood up with his hands in the air in a cluster of rocks above the position. He was jabbering away in Spanish, but it was obvious that he wanted to surrender. He looked like a teenager – a boy, much like ourselves. He was pleading for his life, begging not to be killed. We looked at each other and hesitated. But we weren't having it. We had just been shelled by our own side and had lost several other guys as well as Dave. These bastards had been shooting at us and now this fucker wanted to surrender? A brief argument broke out between us. Somebody shouted, 'Shoot him. Fucking shoot him.' Out of the darkness, another voice replied, 'No, you fucking shoot him.' Then the first voice was even more insistent: 'Shoot him. Fucking shoot him.' While all this was going on, the hope was beginning to fade from the boy's eyes. He must have known what was coming and crumpled to his knees. Finally, somebody threw a tarpaulin over him, shot him, and finished him off with a bayonet. That was it. One less to worry about. Nothing was said as we moved on. Nowadays, they call it the 'fog of war'.

We continued working our way forward in two- or three-man pods, trying to get a feel for who was where. I assumed my position as number two on the Gimpy. Whenever we heard Spanish spoken we would fire into the darkness. As we pushed on, we felt like we were getting on top of them. But then, when we reached the ridge line, one of the guys shouted in alarm, 'They're counter-attacking! They're counter-attacking!' Argies were coming up from the left, round the back of us. We could hear them talking, just round the corner. It was a scary moment. We fell silent and then one of our lads asked in a whisper if we had any grenades. Two lads nodded. They got together and decided to throw everything they had in the direction of the Spanish voices. In the howling wind and pissing rain, they counted to three and tossed their grenades round the corner. There was a huge explosion and then phosphorus from a grenade was blown back over us. Guys were flicking it off themselves with their bayonets before it had a chance to burn through their clothes. But there was no more Spanish chatter.

We carried on in the darkness, ripping off spurts of fire, and then continuing in an eerie silence. Finally, we got together, took a roll call and checked our ammunition. We were perilously low, so I went around begging, borrowing and stealing from our platoon. As dawn broke, we could make out the Argies across the valley heading towards Port Stanley, where the lights had twinkled away throughout the night as if nothing was happening. They were silhouetted against the rising sun and we could see that they were being attacked from another angle and were trying to protect themselves. One of the lads opened up on them as I fed the link ammunition into the Gimpy as fast as I could. It was just like being on the firing range. We couldn't miss. It was a bit of a turkey shoot really. We took out quite a few of them before the gun jammed. I was fiddling with it, trying to free up the mechanism, when a sniper got his sights on us. We were exposed, so we had to jump behind a large rock and hunker down. Splinters of granite and turf were flying up all around us. The rocks seemed to come to life. Bullets were pinging and zinging, showering us with fragments. We felt like every Argie on the island must have had his gun trained on us. At one point a 50-calibre bullet ricocheted off a rock and landed directly, but softly, in the other lad's lap. We looked at the bullet, looked at each other, then burst into laughter as the snipers continued to fire all around us. It was bizarre – here we were laughing our heads off right in the middle of all this death and destruction. We must have looked like madmen. But what else could we do? Our mates started shouting over, 'Come on – fucking blast them! Get that fucking gun going.' They were pinned down, too, and wanted our covering fire, but we were staying put and shouted back: 'Fuck off, you pricks.'

The Argies attempted a half-hearted counter-offensive, but our artillery quickly put paid to that. The firing gradually subsided and when we next caught up with the Argies we could see them in dejected columns walking down to Port Stanley.

We had taken Wireless Ridge at a cost of yet another three dead. The Argies were twenty-five men down. We had also taken all of our other objectives: Tumbledown, Twin Sisters, Mount Longdon and Mount Harriet were all now in British hands. And the Gurkhas were poised to attack Sapper Ridge – the only remaining obstacle between us and Port Stanley. The Argies had moved some of their big guns into the town, and to our disgust they had positioned them among civilian houses. That led to the deaths of three British women – the only civilian casualties of the whole campaign. But it was obvious the game was up. Surrender negotiations were already under way.

Later that day – 14 June – word came down to us that a white flag was flying over Port Stanley. We were desperate to be the first into town. There was a healthy 'cap badge' rivalry between us and the marines – that is what the regimental system is all about. For symbolic reasons, the bosses wanted the cabbage-heads – who had been kicked out by the Argies back at the beginning of April – to return and raise the Union Flag over the islands once again. But there was no way 2 Para were going to be cheated out of our moment of glory. We had been the first battalion ashore, the first battalion to take on the Argies and win a major battle, and we were bloody sure we were going to be the first battalion into Port Stanley. The race was on, but the result was never in doubt. We reached

Stanley's airfield two and a half hours before the cabbage-heads turned up. Happily, ITV and the war correspondent Max Hastings were on hand to record our triumph.

I was pretty shocked by the state of the town. It had obviously been in a war. Some of the buildings were still burning, and stinking corpses were lying in the streets with pieces of tarpaulin, carpet, cardboard, corrugated iron – anything that had come to hand – thrown over them. Other dead Argies had fallen in a stream, and some of our boys got dysentery when they used it for drinking water, not knowing it was polluted. The place was also indescribably filthy. There was human excrement and garbage everywhere. Discipline had obviously broken down some time earlier. There had been widespread vandalism, and for some stupid reason the Argies had decided to blow up the water-pumping station on the day they surrendered. Streets and buildings had been renamed in Spanish – after all, we were in 'Puerto Argentina'. Anti-aircraft guns had been installed in the school playground, and the Argies had painted red crosses on their ammunition stores and officers' billets. That disgusted us even more than the crap in the streets.

The locals gave us an emotional welcome, cheering us as liberators, just as they had in Goose Green. But we were in no mood for a party just yet. We were tired and dirty. Each platoon or company was assigned a house where they could crash out. Some had been used by the occupiers as public toilets so had to be cleaned first, but it was like heaven for us. There was no power for heating, but it was so warm compared to what we had been used to up in the mountains. We were told to unload our weapons and pile our grenades in a corner. There must have been about fifty grenades sitting in a cardboard box, just in case we needed them, because the Argies were still around, mostly camped out on the runway.

After a good rest, we got up the next morning and tried to present ourselves as best we could. We washed with what little water there was, got dressed and assembled on parade to watch the marines come yomping through town and take the surrender. Deep down, we had a lot of respect for them. We knew they were the second-best unit – just below us, of course – but they still got verbal torture from our ranks as they marched past. There was plenty of laughter as they had to keep straight faces while we enquired loudly, 'Oh, you've decided to turn up, have you? What time do you call this? Where the fuck have you been?'

Once the parade was over, we were just starting our clean-up duties when – deep joy – we came across a warehouse full of wine. Cases and cases of plonk. We could not believe our luck. We raced back to our house, emptied our Bergens and charged back to the warehouse to stock up with the bevvy. Suddenly, though, someone yelled, 'Stop!' The whole place was booby-trapped. We took stock, grabbed a few bottles, and headed back to the house. We were just glad nobody had been killed, and at least we had some booty. We opened one or two bottles in celebration but as soon as we took a mouthful we discovered it was vinegar!

On our second or third day in town, we attended a memorial service, with Padre Cooper – the sure-shot sermoniser – doing his bit. We all crowded into Port Stanley Cathedral and listened intently. The padre told us we were not the same people as the ones who had come down on the *Norland* four weeks earlier. Our lives had been changed for ever. 'When you hear the whistle of something coming in and you know it's nasty – or you have got a bit of cover and you know you have to get up and move while somebody is trying to kill you – you begin to understand the priorities in life. When you are faced with these stark realities, you would be a very insensible person if you did not think more profoundly than you ever have in your life before.' He was right, but I don't think many of us realised just how much our lives had been changed. In some cases, it would be many years before we did.

Within forty-eight hours of the surrender, Galtieri was out of power and the repatriation of prisoners was on the agenda. We had six thousand in Stanley alone, and they were a cold and miserable bunch. Most of them were camped out at the airfield in pretty hellish conditions. Over the next few days, we sorted out their munitions. We found piles of rifles, grenades, mortars, all sorts of stuff lying all over the place. It was a laborious task but we were quite happy to do it. It was certainly better than being shot at!

The prisoner handling was all done quite professionally. There was no real animosity towards them now that their mates were no longer trying to kill us. They were a mixture of conscripts and regulars, and the old regulars didn't take too kindly to teenage paras pushing and ordering them around. But if they gave us any attitude, they got short shrift, either with a rifle butt in the belly or a kick up the arse. They were just trying it on.

Some of the conscripts were just kids – eighteen-year-olds. We had eighteen-year-olds, too, but there was a big difference between them and the Argies. Our young lads had joined up because they'd wanted to, then they had gone through selection and the best training in the world. A lot of the Argies had clearly just been told to dig in and hold. Then they had sat there with their rifles, waiting to be told to fire at us. The regulars had set up the minefields and the arcs of fire, but the conscripts had not been up for the fight. We heard stories that the Argentinian special forces had executed some of them after they'd tried to desert. To make matters worse for the Argie top brass, many of the conscripts were from the sub-tropical north of Argentina, so they could not cope with the extreme cold. Galtieri had held back his crack troops – from the colder south of the country – because of an ongoing territorial dispute with Chile.

A lot of the prisoners went back to Argentina on the *Canberra*. That must have been a big surprise for them, because their bosses had told them it had been sunk. As we processed them and loaded them onto the ships, we pinched war trophies in the time-honoured military tradition. Bayonets, compasses and revolvers were all eagerly sought, but their folding Belgian FN rifles were especially prized. I was down at the docks when I saw one prisoner clutching a shiny black box. He was a bit taller than me but around the same age. He looked exhausted. I went over and took the box from him. Inside was a shiny regimental trumpet. I thought it would be a fantastic war trophy so I swiped it. When I got it back to the house, I discovered a little exercise book with a regimental number and the name 'Omar Rene Tabarez'.

The Argies were just as desperate to get off the island as we were. But we would be going home in triumph – as victors – while they were going back to Argentina with the shame of defeat and would come to be regarded as a painful reminder of a national embarrassment. I did not envy them.

Finally, the great day came and, to the delight of Wendy, it was finally our turn to pile aboard the *Norland* and set sail for home. I had a tear in my eye for the lads we were leaving behind, but I clenched my jaw firmly. I was putting the Falklands behind me and would never return to this God-awful place. Or so I thought . . .

CHAPTER 5

GHOSTS OF THE FALKLANDS

We were physically shattered after the Falklands and on that first night back aboard the *Norland* we all conked out and slept for eighteen hours. When we woke up, we were greeted with more bizarre evidence of the extreme exhaustion we were suffering – the whole floor was covered in crap! Guys had got up in the middle of the night with no idea where they were and had taken a dump on the floor. It was disgusting, but it said a lot about the state we were in.

On the voyage back to the Ascension Islands, we were joined on board the *Norland* by the guys from 3 Para – our arch rivals. They had fought hard at Mount Longdon, losing twenty-three guys during the ten-hour battle and the thirty-five hours of shelling that followed. One of them – Sergeant Ian McKay – had been awarded a posthumous Victoria Cross for single-handedly storming an Argie position. We were all in high spirits and the guys from 3 Para were full of even more shit than usual. When the beer was broken out the recipe for disaster was complete. Take two rival battalions of the toughest soldiers in the British Army. Send them into battle for three weeks. Then coop them up on the same ship and fill them full of booze. What began as a colossal piss-up ended in a massive punch-up. Everyone got smashed out of their heads and the evening evolved into one almighty, full-on brawl that had the *Norland*'s stewards cowering under tables and locking themselves in their cabins. It was kind of inevitable for the Parachute Regiment. If we couldn't find anyone else to fight, we would fight one another. And while this might sound weird, it was all done in good humour.

The following morning, the RSM gave us all a good and proper bollocking. We were told not to do it again, but there was a sense of relief that we had got it out of our systems.

From Ascension, we were flown back to RAF Brize Norton, where the army had assembled all our families for a big homecoming. Prince Charles was there to greet us, too. That moment of return was incredibly emotional. Big, tough men had tears rolling down their cheeks when we landed and saw the cheering crowds. It showed how deep our feelings were running and was an early indication of how much our experiences in the Falklands had affected us.

I spotted Mum and Dad among the banner-waving crowds and the Union Flags. Mum had not thought to make a banner, but when she saw the other families with theirs she was not to be outdone. She grabbed a paper plate and wrote just one word in big letters with a black felt-tip pen: 'ANTHONY!' We hugged and then the tears came for me, too. Mum had been scared stiff during the war – every time she'd seen a policeman in the street she'd been frightened that he was coming to her door with bad news. One of our neighbours' brothers, who was serving in the SAS, had been killed at the beginning of the war, so from then on Mum couldn't help but worry about me. Like most of the families, she had been glued to the television and had lived through some grim moments, like the news of the death of Colonel Jones. Now she was crying with relief and I joked with her to cheer her up. When I was wee, she used to tease me about my big nose, so I told her, 'See this nose. It dug a lot of holes in the Falklands.' It was great to be home in one piece and among my loved ones, but I didn't say much on the long drive up to Dundee. I was struck by how normal everything looked and how people were just getting on with their lives. They had no idea what we had seen and been through, and I thought most of them were probably not that interested, either.

During that drive, I decided to try to forget about the war, and it became a bit like a dirty secret for me. It was not so easy to do, though, and I became short-tempered and far too aggressive. I would bite off people's heads for nothing at all – it was my way or the highway. Eventually, Mum sat me down and told me that the war had changed me. She said I might not have been physically wounded in the Falklands, but I had left my heart there. I had become hard and cynical. I was tormented by a cocktail of emotions and harrowing memories. I felt a strange mixture of guilt and anger about the whole thing. I was especially furious about the acclaim being heaped on H Jones – who I felt got his VC for being a stupid upper-class twit. I didn't buy into the idea that the award recognised the achievements of the entire battalion. I was also annoyed that Grayling received a Military Medal just for being there when Bingley was killed while charging an Argie position. What had Grayling done that was more than what we had all done? But I was most angry that Dave Parr, who had returned to the battlefield voluntarily, received no recognition whatsoever – maybe because he was killed by our own side.

Like hundreds of other veterans in both Britain and Argentina, I started drinking heavily, abusing alcohol to cope with my feelings of anger and anxiety. I was on a slippery slope and careered down it at a rapid rate of knots. I drank far, far too much and got into a lot of fights. I didn't like myself for it, but that was how I was. There were times when I would sit on my own with music on, drinking, and thinking, Why did they all have to die? I went through a lot of depression and introspection. I used to question the purpose of this life. I was not religious, but I would wonder what it was all about. The line between becoming an alcoholic or a convict and going on to make something of my life was very, very fine during this period.

By now, I wanted to get out of the army. The fun of playing 'bang-bang-you're-dead' had lost its attraction. I had been impressed by our medics in the Falklands. They had made a difference in an entirely positive way. They had helped people. I was still into fitness and decided that I wanted to get into sports physiotherapy, so a year after I came back from the Falklands I applied to join the Royal Army Medical Corps and then went to Belize on a six-month tour.

Belize was a crazy time. Most of our leave was spent in Raul's Rose Garden, a notorious establishment in the Ladyville suburb of Belize city. There was nothing lady-like in this part of Ladyville. Raul's Rose Garden was one of the most infamous brothels in the history of the British Army. Our medical officer gave the girls a monthly check-up in a desperate but largely futile attempt to stem the rising number of venereal disease cases. Some of the girls were quite beautiful and they were drawn from all over Central America but God knows what kind of diseases were incubated in that place. Raul himself was a bastard and widely hated. He would sit in his big chair half asleep wearing a big fedora hat. But when the inevitable trouble broke out at the bar he would suddenly burst into life wielding a huge sword and start swiping at all and sundry. The girls were never paid directly. Instead the guys paid a teller at a cash desk. By the end of the month we were all broke and Raul was accepting our watches as security. I then hit on an ingenious scheme. Filling stations in the UK at the time were doing promotions on black plastic digital watches which you could buy for £1.99. I got one of my mates in Dundee to send out thirty watches and we had the time of our lives at the Rose Garden. We managed to get through about two dozen watches before Raul twigged and went mental. We were all a bit mental down there; maybe we were still getting the war out of our systems. It was no surprise really that our trip ended in a huge punch-up. We had a bit of rivalry and ongoing friction with the Royal Corps of Transport on the base. They had a long-haired monkey as a mascot. It was a beautiful thing and it was their pride and joy. One day the monkey disappeared. When it was found hanging from the flagpole the balloon went up. The finger of suspicion was fairly pointed at one of our lads in 2 Para. The fight that followed was absolutely epic. I had never seen anything like it. The whole canteen erupted in an explosion of violence. Even the officers and senior NCOs were involved. It was a miracle nobody was killed.

When we got back to Britain I was based at the Keogh Barracks at Ash Vale in Hampshire. I was on an exercise when I was suddenly called off and told to report back to the barracks. When I got back I was given some shattering news. My brother Ernie had been working hard to build up his legal firm. Maybe too hard. The pressure to succeed had been too great and one day he had disappeared. Ernie's body had been found in London. He was a non-swimmer and it seemed he had thrown himself into the Thames. I had to travel to London, report to a police station and identify the body. I was angry that he had taken his own life. He was just thirty-four years of age. How could he do that? I'd hardly known him while growing up, but the whole family had been proud of his success. Of course, Mum and Dad were devastated. But they were insistent that I should not identify Ernie's body on my own. They knew that I had been deeply affected by seeing my mates killed in the Falklands and they insisted that Roddy travel down from Dundee to be with me when we identified the body. I slept in a police cell overnight, waiting for Roddy to arrive. In the morning when I woke up Roddy was there. I had seen far too many dead bodies already, and this time it would be my own brother's. We went through the grim formalities of identifying Ernie and signing the paperwork. On the train back to Dundee, I got pissed and all sorts of thoughts ran through my mind. I was smouldering with anger, resentment and bewilderment. When I got home, I punched a hole in the living-room wall and poor old Mum had to hang a picture over it.

Coming so soon after the Falklands, Ernie's death really put me on the skids. I had no idea what I was trying to cope with. Unknown to me, some super-tough soldiers had gone to see psychiatrists after the war. If post-traumatic stress disorder could affect battle-hardened warriors like that, it could certainly affect twenty-year-olds like me and my mates. And it did. All over Britain – and in Argentina – veterans were abusing drink and drugs, with many winding up in jail. Others who had survived the war did not survive the peace. In Argentina, the number of veterans who killed themselves would eventually surpass the number of soldiers killed in the land fighting. And many of our own lads suffered in exactly the same way and ultimately took their own lives. Suicide was the silent killer of the South Atlantic.

I never really talked to anyone about my feelings, so I thought I was alone. My wild drinking started to get really out of control. One weekend, just before New Year, I went back to Dundee on leave and met up with Gary Whyte and Stewart Hutchison, my old mates from 15 Para, the territorials based at St Andrews. They were waiting for me at the train station and we went straight out on the bevvy. We were boozing like there was no tomorrow, and for some crazy reason we decided to go off and join the French Foreign Legion. Running away – from the army and my memories of the Falklands – sounded like a great idea at the time, so I went absent without leave and we took the train and ferry over to Lille – where the Legion has its main recruiting base for the north of France. It was all very James Bond, very hush-hush. We knocked on a secret door and were taken one by one into a room where we were thoroughly questioned. Next we were sent on an overnight train to Paris and then down to the Legion's headquarters in Marseille. By the time we arrived, they knew everything about us. They had fully checked out our stories and had amassed an amazing amount of extra information, too. We were grilled again in Marseille, but while I was waiting to see if they would accept me, Gary took me aside and told me, 'Go home, Tony. I can go back home whenever. But if you desert and try to go back, you'll be arrested.'

They were right, so I reluctantly went back to Britain. I was arrested on my return, but luckily escaped jail. I think the army had already learned that they had to cut Falklands veterans a bit of slack. They'd been happy with my performance down in the South Atlantic, and they wanted to keep me in. So I was sent to the Paramedic Field Ambulance medics in the Airborne Brigade. From there, I was posted to Canada for extra training. It was great. We learned a fair bit and the duties were not too onerous. Most of our cases involved Gurkhas who had come out with us. They would come into the clinic, point at their crotch and complain, 'Sore pee pee.' We would nod, tell them their nocturnal adventures had caught up with them and call them 'dirty wee bastards'.

Unfortunately, the drink was pretty cheap in Canada and I got steamed in about it. Invariably, these booze-ups ended in trouble. One night, we were doing a pub crawl with some local Indian guys who were driving us around. Every pub was so far away from the next one that you needed a car. But when we were well and truly pissed, the Indians tried to mug us. That was a big mistake. The Battle of Little Big Horn was replayed in a pub car park, but this time the Indians lost. We gave them such a hiding that they ended up in hospital.

After my stint in Canada, I went to meet Gary in Paris to see how he was getting on in the Legion. We hit the town with a load of other Legionnaires. They were at the peak of fitness and vast quantities of drink went down. The festivities came to a swift halt, however, when we entered a bar full of leather-jacketed bikers. It must have been one of the greatest pub brawls of all time – the French Foreign Legion versus the Hell's Angels. Naturally, I pitched in on the side of the Legion. The gendarmes did not appreciate the historic nature of the battle, though, and when they arrived at the smashed-up pub I once again found myself under arrest. Fortunately, the Legion pulled some strings and after eighteen hours of playing cards with illegal Polish immigrants we were out.

On my next continental trip to meet Dundee's answer to Beau Geste we decided it was best to avoid crowds, but that didn't stop us getting into trouble. We met in Oostende and got well and truly pissed sampling Belgium's famous beers. Finding ourselves locked out of the hotel, we decided to break in – but unfortunately we picked the wrong room. That was it. Now we were under arrest for breaking and entering and we saw the inside of a Belgian nick.

My career as an international wild man seemed to be progressing nicely, but it culminated back home in Dundee. I got involved in a fight at a taxi rank after a day on the drink and a night in the disco. That led to yet another night in the cells, but this time I wasn't let off with a warning – I had to go to court. I was as guilty as sin and did not look forward to going into the dock with two black eyes and skinned knuckles. Luckily, though, I secured the services of Dundee's top criminal lawyer, William G. Boyle. He was a great supporter of the military and a friend of my late brother. He liked to be called 'Mr Boyle', but he was universally known to Dundee's sizeable criminal fraternity as 'Billy'. When my turn came, I shuffled shamefaced into the dock and Billy got to his feet. I was in awe of his performance. He was brilliant. I came across as an angel with a dirty face and a war hero who had been minding my own business when I was set upon for no reason by a bunch of good-for-nothings. Billy was so convincing that I almost began to believe I was innocent myself. When he sat down the sheriff looked severe. He gave a cough and sifted through his notes for what seemed like an eternity. Then he looked at me and uttered the immortal words: 'I find you not guilty. You are discharged from the dock.'

I did not enjoy my court appearance and my brush with the law was a bit of a wake-up call. It was reported in the local evening newspaper and Mum and Dad were mortified. I decided it was time to bury my Falklands experiences, shut them out of my mind, shelve them and move on. I had to get myself sorted and settle down.

Unfortunately, by now, the military had closed the Joint Services Corps of Physiotherapy, so my ambition to train within the army to become a physiotherapist was scuppered. The careers advisers suggested I might try radiography instead, so I was sent to Queen Elizabeth's Hospital in Woolwich, London. It was the first time in a while that I had been challenged mentally. And there were nurses there! The disco on a Thursday night in the NAAFI was not to be missed. One Friday, hung over, a mate looked out the window and neatly summed it up. He saw a group of nurses walking across the quadrangle and said in a Churchillian accent, 'Never have so few given so much to so many!'

The training was good fun, but limited. Speaking to some Far East prisoners of war who were still receiving treatment after their ordeals at the hands of the Japanese in the Second World War was interesting – they were great old boys. But radiography was not something I wanted to do for the rest of my life. All I did was X-rays. I never treated anyone or fixed anything. I needed to be part of that end product. I was ready to move on again.

By now, I had found romance with Alison, an army nurse who I met at one of those Thursday night discos. She was sitting at the bar, with a lovely pair of legs, and I thought, She's the one for me. I chased her relentlessly, but she would not have anything to do with me for a long time. She was from an upper-class family, while I was a wee working-class laddie from Dundee. She could not possibly take me home. But I was mad keen on her and would not give up. I just refused to take no for an answer. Eventually, she caved in and we started going out together.

Meeting her family was a bit daunting, but I could hold my own in their circle. I could socialise and talk the talk. While I was not a great book reader, I read the newspapers, watched television documentaries and had a good general knowledge, so I was reasonably well informed and could hold a conversation on a range of subjects with some ease. Because of Dad's background in the RAF, I also knew how to conduct myself in a formal situation – starting with the cutlery on the outside and working your way in, tipping the soup plate away from myself, all that stuff.

Alison's father was one of the huntin', shootin' and fishin' set, but he was a really great guy and I got on very well with him. He flew his own light aircraft – a personal ambition of mine, too – and took me to his local airfield one day. There was a fifty-six-gallon drum which had to be moved, so I just picked it up and moved it. Under his breath, he said, 'Strong, if nothing else.' He owned a tool-hire business and eventually offered me a job, but I turned him down. I said I wanted to be my own man, which I think he respected, because he could tell I didn't want to hang on to his coat-tails. The day I won him over was when we were in their massive country house on the Welsh Borders and he sent me down to the wine cellar to pick a bottle for the evening meal. You could write what I knew about wine on the back of a postage stamp, so I was in a bit of a flap. I went down and scratched my head, trying to read these labels written in foreign languages. Then, after a while, it dawned on me – I'd just go for the one with the most dust on it, as that would obviously be his most precious bottle. I brought it back to the table and showed him. He had no choice but to smile and say, 'Very good. A very good choice.' He couldn't say no.

Their lifestyle opened my eyes to real wealth. I was introduced to the London scene and was dining with aristocrats. It really boosted my confidence when I found that I could talk easily with them.

I was twenty-five when we got married. I still intended to do a physiotherapy course, but I had to wait ten months, so as a stop-gap my old mate Wayne Rees from the Falklands got me a job with him selling life insurance in Aldershot. It was a bit different from the last time we had worked together – on the Gimpy shooting Argies. We never spoke much about the war, and certainly never discussed how it had affected us. Unknown to me, Wayne was suffering from unsettling dreams and, just like me, he had become short-tempered, intolerant and aggressive. It was a hard-sell job, but I worked out that if I got four appointments a day, I could make a thousand quid a month – a lot of money in 1987. Before long, I realised I was pretty good at it. The paras had given me a very task-orientated outlook. If you failed to finish things in the army, you were a goner. The training was very tough, but it gave you direction and confidence. Paras are constantly told they are the best, so I had no doubt that I would be a success in the insurance business, too. I've always been scared of failure, which drives me to succeed. I'm an all-or-nothing guy. If I'm in it, I'm in it all the way. So selling was not so hard, and rejection did not bother me. It was just a numbers game.

The motto of the paras' training school has always stuck with me: 'Knowledge Dispels Fear'. I believe that if you have the knowledge, you will always be fine. But now I added two more mottos to my business philosophy, and I've kept to them ever since: the paras' regimental motto, '*Utrinque Paratus*' – 'Ready for Anything' – and the motto of the Royal Army Medical Corps, 'Steadfast in Adversity'.

There was a lot of cold calling involved in selling insurance, which meant going through the phone book. But since I had been in the army, knew a lot of folk and was part of the 'Dundee mafia', I also had a lot of personal contacts to sell to. The office was quite a macho environment, which suited me. It was 'sell, sell, sell'. You were not allowed to sit down.

I was determined and very persistent. I soon learned that women were the key to the deals. If you got them on side, they would hen-peck the husband until he relented. I would say things like, 'Well, madam, you appear to be a very sensible person, but obviously your husband doesn't want to pay for your security. Good day.' She would usually be on the phone in a few days. Before long, I was making three or four thousand pounds every month. The bosses wanted me to open some more branches for them and have guys underneath me, which I told them I was happy to do, as long as it was in Scotland. They didn't like that, and as punishment for getting above my station, they sent me to Croydon, a place I detested.

I set up a new branch there with a former PE teacher called Paul Hearn. He was a good bloke and our ethos was: recruit, train, motivate and sell.

But living and working in Croydon only increased my desire to get out of London. Alison was pregnant with our first child, Emma, and I asked her what she wanted to do: move to near her parents or head up to Scotland to be near mine? She had been at finishing school with a daughter of the DC Thomson publishing dynasty, so she already knew some people in Tayside. Her father was always up in Scotland, too – fishing on the Tay, Dee and Spey, spending a fortune on all the great salmon rivers. She said she was happy to relocate to Scotland and we made the move. We sold our house in Aldershot literally a month before the big property crash of 1989. We were very lucky to make a good bit of money on it – about £50,000. At the same time, Alison's father decided to sell the family business, and as a result she received £150,000 as an early inheritance.

In Dundee, I got a job with another insurance company, which would give us an income while we decided what sort of business we wanted to set up for ourselves. We stayed with my sister Terry, who had a flat on Arbroath Road, basically camping in her home until we found somewhere to buy. I did not want to live in the city – I wanted to make a fresh start and much preferred the surrounding countryside, which is very beautiful. We looked at lots of places in all sorts of different areas until we settled on a wee cottage near Kirriemuir, a small town at the mouth of the Angus glens that is famed as the birthplace of *Peter Pan* creator J. M. Barrie.

We wanted to start a family business and we identified nursing homes as a possibility. The population was ageing and there was clearly a growing market. We also felt that we could make a difference. The quality of care homes at the time was pretty poor and we felt that we could do better. Margaret Thatcher had recently introduced legislation that had changed all the rules for the sector, and she wanted the NHS to close all of its old care homes. Duncan Bannatyne, the multi-millionaire from the hit TV series *Dragons' Den*, had already spotted the same window of opportunity. He tells a brilliant story about filling his first care home with his mum's elderly mates before the bank manager came around for an inspection, so he could say, 'We're full!' That allowed him to get the money to fund his next home.

I needed time to investigate how to set up a care home, and in the meantime I got a job on the rigs, working as a paramedic. I did survival training at the Robert Gordon Institute of Technology in Aberdeen, but my first shift wasn't out in the wild North Sea but in Invergordon, where the rig was parked for refurbishment. I just had to sit there while it was being worked on, but at least that gave me plenty of time for research.

Even now, I was still haunted by ghosts of the Falklands. Anyone who goes to war and sees people shot and blown up cannot fail to be affected by it. Different events and news items would trigger disturbing thoughts. The Gulf War broke out in August 1990 and it all came flooding back. As the troops flew out, I remembered our departure from Portsmouth and the guys we lost down in the Falklands. I would think of Steve Dixon, Dave Parr, the young Argie who had tried to surrender, and all the other boys who had died down there. I was angry and bitter, but still kept everything bottled up. I felt I was the only one going through it. I was unaware that thousands of veterans were experiencing similar turmoil and that some of them were going through absolute hell with post-traumatic stress.

Then, in 1990, Roddy died of a brain tumour. Just like Ernie, he was only thirty-four when he died. By the end, he was like a bag of bones – barely recognisable as the brother who had been so full of fun. My father was devastated. This was the second son he'd had to bury, and he never got over it.

A few months later, my old pal Gary Whyte was killed while serving in Djibouti with the Foreign Legion. I felt like the Grim Reaper – anyone near me seemed to end up dead. Gary was blown up. He was on double mortars when his mate put the second one in too quickly and blew Gary to pieces. I helped to bring the body back home and organise the funeral, which was a military affair because Gary had been in the TA, but I could not force myself to enter the church. I just couldn't take any more. I felt guilty because I'd left him in Marseille. Of course, it had been his choice to join the Legion, but I couldn't see it that way at the time and I took his death very hard.

My coping mechanism was to focus totally on the business and throw myself into it 100 per cent. I blocked out everything else. That allowed me to get through a very depressing period, at least to some extent. I thought I could shut down my emotions and escape the ghosts of the Falklands by keeping myself busy. I suppose it was a very male reaction. I did not realise that I was not dealing with things – I was simply postponing having to deal with them. I plunged into planning the care home business, joined the local Round Table, met my mate Bill Milne, who is still working with me now, and got networking. One day, I was meant to go to Auchterarder to look at a possible care home when Bill phoned me. His brother-in-law, a surveyor, had spotted a house in Kirriemuir that was up for sale. It sounded promising, so I went round the corner to have a look. Lisden House was a spectacular old Victorian mansion, complete with Gothic turrets, a stable block and outbuildings. It was built out of red sandstone and looked awesome – more like a castle than a house.

I was excited. I could envisage building extensions and

turning the attic into a family flat. At the time, I never thought about building a brand-new home from scratch. In hindsight, that is probably what I should have done, but back then all care homes seemed to be old mansion houses – the new-build thing had not really taken off. As soon as I got home, I got in touch with an architect. We arranged to go and look at it together, and he agreed it could be a goer. The house was originally built in the Scots baronial style by the wealthy Wilkie family, who were textile barons. The owner prior to us was a guy called Barry Lawson, who used to run the Timex factories in Dundee.

Through the Round Table, I met a local accountant who put me in touch with a bank. In those days, you could actually go and meet your local bank manager and talk sensibly with them. Decisions were taken locally and often on a basis of trust, at least to a certain extent. Alison and I had about £150,000 to put in, and the bank loaned us about £750,000, which was pretty unheard of at the time and would certainly never happen now. We did the deal on 31 August 1991. The planning permission came through and we started work straight away. Bill worked at a building company, and we gave them the contract to fit out the home.

Everything we had was in the venture, so we decided to move into the building to keep a close eye on the work. We sold our cottage and moved into the lounge, with its huge high ceiling and ornate cornicing. Alison, baby Emma and myself lived in that one room. Boxes of stuff were piled up all around us, and the place was always full of builders hammering away with dust flying about. I was on site every day and was flat out. We had to meet the required standards but I wanted to exceed them. We had to get the place registered, hire staff and source suppliers. It never stopped. Dad came down every night after he finished work to check on what the builders had been up to that day.

There were thirty-one bedrooms, each with an en suite toilet, which at the time was quite cutting edge, but we wanted to make the place special. As the opening date neared, everyone chipped in, with Mum and Dad and Alison's parents helping us clean up. We converted the attic into a two-bedroom flat, accessed by the back stairs, and moved in as soon as it had been completed.

I was only twenty-nine at the time. I think some locals viewed the project quite suspiciously, wondering how this young lad had managed to achieve all this, especially as Lisden was *the* house in Kirriemuir.

We opened Lisden Care Home in April 1992, with Alison acting as the matron. All of the local worthies turned up – ministers, priests, councillors, even the provost came to have a glass of sherry and a sandwich. Our first resident was there, too. I had personally gone round to his house in Kirriemuir.

to persuade him to come in. Thereafter, I did the same thing several more times – visiting family homes to convince people to come and stay with us. It was bizarre. I would never do something like that now, but I had to do it then. I knew the business model inside out and was acutely aware of our projections of how many people we needed to make it work. For a time, that occupied all my time. I did not dwell on the deaths of Roddy and Gary, and thoughts of the war rarely intruded into my mind. I kept myself busy . . . and kept the ghosts at bay.

By September, the place was running well. We were starting to fill the rooms. Then Black Wednesday happened. On 16 September, Britain plunged into the European Exchange Rate Mechanism Crisis. The UK had entered the ERM two years earlier, but the government was forced to exit when the Treasury – under Chancellor Norman Lamont – lost approximately £3.4 billion in one day. The previous day, the Bank of England's base interest rate had been 10 per cent. By the end of Black Wednesday, it was 15 per cent. I listened in horror to the car radio as it all unravelled, muttering, 'We may as well throw the keys into the bank on our way past.' I sat there sweating, glued to the coverage, thinking our business was now totally unsustainable. Despite all our best work, it seemed we were sure to go down the Swanny. But the next day the interest rate went back down to 10 per cent and the crisis was over. We had escaped by the skin of our teeth.

Over the next year, Lisden House really filled up and we were soon running at full occupancy. We had acquired quite a bit of land with the property, so I started to look into what we might do with it. I applied for planning permission to build some private sheltered housing in the grounds, with the idea that this would be a feeder to the main care home. I thought I could sell them and use the profits to fund a second care home, but I soon learned that there was no real market for private sheltered housing back then.

Around this time, the government raised VAT from 15 to 17.5 per cent. I remember thinking, You bastards. You've just added 2.5 per cent to my costs, because we couldn't reclaim the VAT. Then the architect told me that we *could* claim it back if Lisden House was a listed building. It wasn't at the time, but I soon made sure it was. I phoned Historic Scotland – or whatever the agency was called at the time – and convinced them to come and look at it. The official told me, 'We hardly ever get anyone wanting us to list their properties. It's usually people trying to get them unlisted.' I laid it on thick: 'Look at this wonderful building. It's over a hundred years old, you know. Just look at that beautifully crafted staircase . . .' We got the listing, so we were able to claim back the VAT, but it proved to be a double-edged sword. Every time we applied for planning permission, we also had to get listed-building consent, which was often a major headache.

We ended up selling the extra land to a housing association, which gave us enough money to go and look for something else. I heard that Perth and Kinross Council was seeking to offload some of its care homes and went to look at one in Perth. I reckoned it was a no-brainer to expand the business and buy another care home. We had the model, we knew it worked, so, with a bit of work and planning, we could make it work again. Alison wasn't happy about branching out, though. She did not want to develop the business. She wanted just one home, a small family business. It would tick away and we would live happily ever after. I could not settle for that. I would have too much time on my hands. Running a single home did not interest me. In fact, it bored me. I didn't want the business to grow in a huge way, but I did want more than we had. I also wanted to keep busy. I felt that standing still was like going backwards. My ambition greatly outstripped hers. Alison's vision of a quiet home life and my habit of constantly putting work first began to put a strain on our relationship.

I vividly remember the day when I went to see the home in Perth with the architect. It was in a great location – near the River Tay, beside the Black Watch's regimental headquarters. Called Balhousie Castle, it would eventually provide the inspiration for my business name – the Balhousie Care Group. But the building itself was stinking, dingy and horrible – typical of an old local authority home at the time. Afterwards, the architect and I sat in his car and discussed how much to bid. I did not have a clue. This side of the business was alien to me. We decided to go in with a really low offer and, much to my surprise, we ended up getting it. The architect was as excited as I was.

Again, the building needed a lot of refurbishment to bring it up to scratch, but in 1997 we finally reopened it as North Inch House. The great attraction, aside from getting it at a good price, was that it was already a care home – and it was full of residents. The council could not move them out, because it did not have anywhere else to put them. The only problem was that we were saddled with the old council employees during a three-month transition period while we recruited our own staff. We had to pay them while the council found them new jobs. The thinking was that this would make the transition as smooth as possible for the residents, but it was a real pain for us. The council workers were earning substantially more than our own staff, and obviously they were very keen to shout about it. I had no control over what they did because they were not really my staff. Typical civil servants – they were getting double- and triple-time for shift work and I was paying for it! It was a long three months, and I was glad when I finally got the last one out of the door.

North Inch House also came with a plot of land beside it, as well as a smaller house that had once been the manager's home but was now being used as council offices. When I bought the main building, I ensured that I had right of pre-emption over the smaller house – which meant the council could not sell it without offering it to me first. That turned out to be a smart move, because down the line I bought it at a bargain price and turned it into another care home.

North Inch soon proved to be as big a success as Lisden, and that boosted my confidence. I knew the market, I knew how to handle the inspectors, the local authorities and the planners, so I felt I should move forward. I was always look-ing for an opportunity to expand. I would speak to land agents and ask them to give me a heads-up whenever anything with potential came on the market. If they ever phoned about a place, the first thing I'd say would be: 'Send me the accounts.' That used to annoy them, because they always wanted me to go and look at it first. But I always insisted on seeing the accounts before the building. I had a model in my head and the numbers would tell me if it would work. I could see where people were overspending – start-up costs should be no more than X; heating, lighting and ancillaries should be no more than Y – and if they all stacked up, I would base my fig-ures on 80 per cent occupancy – rather than 100 per cent – so I had some leeway, just in case there were any problems. It would have to be seriously bad to achieve only 80 per cent, so if the figures still added up, I was happy and would go and check out the building.

Once I had looked at a place, I would work out where I could add value to it. Could I get planning permission for an extension? Could I increase the number of rooms? If there was no way to add value, I wasn't interested. I was tenacious about planning. I never gave up. With planning permission, if you keep going long enough, you will eventually get it by finding the right angle.

I was completely driven and dedicated. But my focus on the business was taking its toll on my marriage. Our family had grown through the nineties. Emma was born in July 1990, Tom in April 1992 and Robbie in May 1995. Alison enjoyed family life. We had bought a nice house in Kirriemuir and she had stopped working at Lisden House to look after the kids. As the years went on and the business grew, her involvement decreased until she had nothing to do with the care homes at all. It reached the point where I did not want her near the business because I thought she would interfere. In 1999, after twelve years of marriage, we parted company. It was not an amicable split – at the time, she hated my guts. But we speak now for the sake of the kids. Throughout our marriage, there were times when I would rather go out with my mates and get pissed, or sit on my own chewing over business deals until

3 a.m. Although I had always liked having people around me, I could also be very insular.

Just before we split up, I attended a course in Boston run by business gurus from Harvard. One of the speakers was an American Jewish guy nicknamed 'the Rottweiler'. He went all over the world with an asset-stripping business, so his job was to sack people as ruthlessly as possible. He told us one story about shutting a factory in South America and then having to travel to the airport under armed guard.

After the lecture, the first question he asked me was: 'How are you going to pay off your wife?'

I was sitting with some bankers from the Royal Bank of Scotland, so I said, 'Hopefully, the bank will help me out.'

The Rottweiler turned to the bankers and asked, 'Will you?'

They nodded, which seemed to satisfy the Rottweiler. Then he turned to me and said, 'What you need to do is expand, and as quickly as possible. Don't worry about it. Sure, there's government interference and all that crap. But you know how to deal with that, and they need you more than you need them. And the bank will lend you money to allow you to do it. Won't you, guys?' The bankers all nodded furiously.

I thought this guy was a top man, and I decided to take his advice there and then. Throughout the nineties, it had very much been a lifestyle business for me. Now I was pushing forty and thought I could do a lot better. I suppose it was a bit of a midlife crisis. At that stage, I had a lot of confidence to go forward and make a real go of it, so the Rottweiler's words were music to my ears.

In 2001 I suffered another personal blow when my father died at the age of seventy-four. He had suffered with heart trouble for a few years and his condition was worsening. He was recommended to have surgery. I was not keen on it and felt he should struggle on without it but Dad opted to give it a go. I took him up to the hospital in Aberdeen for the operation. We are not a very touchy-feely family but as I was leaving him on the ward, I turned back and gave him a hug. I suppose I must have subconsciously thought that he might not make it.

When they opened him up, the surgeons found that his heart had deteriorated badly. There was nothing to work with and he died on the table. We received a phone call telling us there had been complications and we had better make our way to Aberdeen. Both Terry and I knew what that meant and I think my mum did as well. However, all the way up to the hospital she kept saying, 'He'll be all right. He'll be all right.' When we arrived we were given the bad news.

Mum and Terry went in to see him but I could not go in. I had seen enough of dead bodies and after having to look at my brother Ernest lying dead, I did not want to do it again to another family member! At his funeral we played Dad's favourite song, 'Somewhere Over the Rainbow'. He loved that song and Judy Garland. As I read my speech, people gasped when I said that I was proud to be burying my dad. But I duly explained that it was right that a son should bury his father and that my dad had experienced the worst pain ever in having to bury two sons. He never ever, ever got over having to do that and the pain of the loss was always with him. To this day Terry and I miss him so, so much.

After Dad's death I really threw myself into building my work. It was a way of coping. Between 2003 and 2011, I opened another nineteen care homes. I was completely driven and poured all my energy into building the business. But my parents never really appreciated my success. When things were going really well with the business, turning over £3 million, before Dad died, he would say to me, 'Don't you think you should go and get a degree?' To him, education was still the main thing.

I would ask, 'Dad, why would I want to go and get a degree now?'

'You would make a good lawyer, son,' he'd say.

Neither he nor Mum could get their head around how big the business had become. And 'debt' was still a dirty word to them. In their world, you saved up for everything. To this day,

Mum still asks me, 'Why are you doing this? You're nearly fifty, you know. Slow down.' And do what? Die?

Deep down, I'm sure they were very proud of me, but they never actually told me. I've never had a 'well done' in my life. When I got five 'A's, a 'B' and a 'C' in my O Grades, my father said, 'Why didn't you get seven "A"s?' I suppose that's just the way it was with Scottish working-class fathers. But it could be quite weird going to a family gathering when one of my aunties would come up to me and say, 'Oh, Anthony, your parents are awfully proud of you.' It always came as a shock. 'Really? Why didn't they tell *me*?'

One thing we do is hire a local cinema for Balhousie conferences and bus in all the staff. The first time we organised one of these, the marketing manager suggested I should invite along my mum. That took me by surprise, but I thought it was a good idea. Afterwards, she said, 'Oh, Anthony, I never realised what a big company you have.' It seemed strange to me that she had never realised the scale of things prior to that day.

Nevertheless, I was on top of the world. My company was successful and I was enjoying my role as chairman. Awards for entrepreneurship brought recognition and I was even in demand as a motivational speaker. I set up a charitable trust to support worthwhile projects, but I was also enjoying the trappings of wealth. I had attained my pilot's licence and flew my own helicopter. I travelled around the globe, trekking through mountains, sky-diving and scuba-diving. I had also met Maggie, my new partner. In short, I had sorted myself out.

Then, in 2009, came a phone call from a television company that would change the course of my life. It would take me back to the Falklands and force me to confront my demons.

CHAPTER 6

SECRET MILLIONAIRE

When I received a phone call out of the blue from a *Secret Millionaire* programme researcher, at first I thought it was a wind-up – maybe one of my mates taking the mickey. But they eventually managed to convince me that it was the real thing and I gave them a hearing. I was non-committal at first because I was really unsure whether it was something I wanted to do. I said I would get back to them and went home and discussed it with family and friends. They all pointed out that there was no downside. And they all asked, 'What are you frightened of, Tony?' As far as I knew, I was not frightened of anything. So I took their comments as a challenge and agreed to do it. Maggie thought it would do me good. She is a transformational life coach with an international clientele and had long suggested that I was not in touch with my feelings.

A researcher duly arrived at my house with a small hand-held camera and we did an interview on my life and background. On the basis of that, the director and producer decided to go ahead with the programme. It was only then that I began to wonder, 'What have I got myself into?'

I had watched and liked *Secret Millionaire* ever since it started. In fact, it is one of my favourite shows. It is always a tear-jerker because it is designed to bring out emotion. The subjects are usually self-made millionaires – ordinary people who have come up the hard way. They are generally not tycoons who were born with a silver spoon and a limited ability to empathise. These successful business people are then confronted by situations and communities where people are striving to help each other and make a difference, often with very little in the way of official support. It is a good concept and I knew that unless you were a really hard bugger, the programme makers would try to get to you somehow.

The director came up to my house at Kirriemuir and the first day's filming of scene-setting shots – the house, the family, where I live, what I do for a living – were done there. Then we flew to Manchester. There has been a lot of adverse publicity in recent years about 'fixing' reality television programmes. That was certainly not the case with *Secret Millionaire*. All I had to agree to do in advance was donate a minimum sum of money at the end of the day, which I felt was fair enough. We stayed in a hotel in Manchester, had dinner and met the rest of the crew – the camera and sound people. I went to bed that night still not having a clue what I was letting myself in for.

In the morning, we went straight to Manchester Piccadilly Station, had a coffee and did some more filming. Then the director turned to me and said, 'Right, now, I had better tell you where you're going. I'll give you a clue – your train is at 11.07 a.m.'

I looked up at the departures board and saw that several trains were scheduled to leave at 11.07. They were going all over the country.

'Birmingham?' No.

'Bristol?' No.

'London?' No.

They finally put me out of my misery: 'Liverpool.'

I was quite happy about that. I had always felt an affinity with Scousers because of the link between Celtic and Liverpool Football Club. Both Glasgow and Liverpool have big Catholic populations. Other than that, though, my knowledge of the city was limited – I knew it had once been an important sea-port and was the home of the Beatles and Cilla Black, but that was about it. I had only ever been to Anfield Stadium at night to watch a game and had left promptly after the final whistle.

On the train, I tried to imagine what Liverpool was going to be like. I thought that it would probably have all the usual problems of a run-down inner city, so I braced myself. When we arrived, they told me I was going to the Anfield area. I was not too alarmed by that, as I had no idea just how run down and rough the district around the Liverpool ground had become. I was soon to learn. The first inkling came when I asked two winos for directions. They were the first people I'd met in Liverpool and one of them turned out to be a Scottish alcoholic! The pair of them were very helpful, but they strongly warned me to watch my wallet. That made me think. Even the down-and-outs were scared of this place.

I was still shocked when I arrived in Anfield, though. The whole place seemed boarded up, with street after street of empty two-up, two-down, late nineteenth-century red-brick terraced houses. It looked like an old *Coronation Street* set – one that had been abandoned decades ago. Quite a few of the houses had been burned out, and the few surviving shops had more security than Fort Knox. So this is inner-city Britain in the twenty-first century, I thought. Bloody hell! It was like Beirut. I was brought up in poverty, but inner-city Dundee in the sixties was very different. For a start, we had hope. People did not burn down their own houses and there were no drugs. I had not seen somewhere like this for years.

The film crew took me to the abandoned house where I would be staying. It was a terrible stinking hole. A mountain of mail had collected behind the door on the filthy, stained carpet, and I put a foot through the rotting floorboards when I walked down the hall. I am quite obsessive about cleanliness. I like things tidy and ordered. I have a spirit-level app on my iPhone and I go round the house checking the paintings are level. I arrange the plates and bowls in the dishwasher so everything is cleaned properly. Maggie sometimes asks me if I feel better for doing it, and I say, 'Yes, darling, I feel great.' I know she's taking the mickey out of me, and other people say that I suffer from obsessive compulsive disorder. They're probably right, but it's just the way I am. So that house was a real shock for me.

The director was pretty hard-nosed. He worked his crew – and me – very hard. He insisted on shots being taken again and again. I could see that he wanted to make the programme as good as it could be, but it drove us nuts. The crew did nothing but complain about him all day long. I finally collared him one morning and said, 'Your crew doesn't stop moaning. This is tough enough for me without having to listen to them whingeing all the time. And do you know what they're moaning about? *You.* If I treated my people the way you're treating them, they wouldn't last very long.' But my objections did not cut much ice with him. He was much respected in the industry – he'd won awards – so he could just carry on.

Making the programme was incredibly stressful. I was introduced to several projects and individuals who were disadvantaged in some way. I was prepared for that, but not for living in Anfield. The local kids amused themselves with arson, and sure enough, during my first night in my temporary home, a house went up in flames. I joined anxious neighbours in the street and watched as the fire brigade doused the blaze. It was shocking – there were fires every night, so it was impossible to feel safe and secure. I just could not get any rest. I nicknamed Anfield 'Vampire City' because you do not see many people during the day – just at night, when all the nutcases, druggies and drunks come out to play. I felt sorry for the good people who were trapped in this hell-hole. And you could tell they were there from their neatly painted doors and window frames and hanging baskets that stuck out like beacons of decency in a decaying landscape. These people had been promised regeneration for years, but instead they had been forced to witness the sad destruction of a once-proud working community.

I had hardly settled in to the house when I made the mistake of leaving on the immersion heater. The electricity was cut off and the meter showed a colossal bill of over forty-five pounds – a sum I could not afford on the meagre budget the programme makers had given me. I was being penalised for running out of electricity. 'Welcome to the poverty trap,' I thought. I spent the night in darkness in a house with bars on the windows. I felt like I'd been incarcerated, but I would have been safer in prison. When I went to stay the night in a local bed and breakfast, I was warned by the tough landlady: 'No brassers [prostitutes] and no bed-wetting.' Salubrious or what?

Eventually, we had to move out of the Anfield house and into a hotel after the crew's vehicles came under attack from a gang of local kids. This was the first time the programme makers had ever been forced to leave an area. It was not a safe environment for any of us. It felt lawless. I could feel the pressure building within me, but I could tell the director was getting a bit upset because I was not showing any emotion. Screw him, I thought, I don't need to go around wearing my heart on my sleeve. I was not built that way. Or so I thought.

The projects in Liverpool, and the people who ran them,

were inspirational. They made me feel humble. I realised just what a privileged position I was in as a wealthy man. They had few or no resources but they were doing their best, not sitting around feeling sorry for themselves. I chose to help out at a charity called DAISY UK, which ran inclusive sporting clubs for disabled kids, their friends and families. It also created work opportunities for long-term unemployed people. This was the other face of Liverpool – compassionate, warm, caring and committed. It was run by Dave Kelly, a real salt-of-the-earth guy with a great sense of humour. He described himself as 'a blind man with a vision'. Fate, he said, had dealt him a million-to-one chance ... but it was not a lottery win. At the age of thirty, he had developed a rare eye condition and lost his sight. His world had been turned upside down but he decided to react positively and trained as a sports coach for the disabled. He saw the need to create sporting opportunities for disabled kids and set up DAISY, which stands for Disability Awareness Introducing Sport to Youngsters. The kids clearly loved Dave, and the unemployed volunteers regained the self-esteem and respect they had lost from being out of work. Working with him made me realise how little I had to complain about in my life. All my little bitches and moans amounted to nothing when compared to the adversity these people had to face every day.

One day, I spotted a van from a charity called Helping Hands and decided to find out more about them. When I learned that one of their activities was to provide help and support for elderly people, I approached them and asked if I could be of any help. Before long, I was accompanying the charity's organiser, Brenda Dodd, on a visit to the home of Jo Allan. She had been a land girl during the Second World War and had lost her husband in 1966 after seventeen years of marriage. She still loved her late husband and felt spiritually close to him, but now she was all on her own and had nobody to help her. It was very sad, especially as she was such a lovely old lady. She was saddled with a huge garden that had become an overgrown jungle. It was a worry and she could no longer take any pleasure from it.

Meeting Jo made me think about my own family life and situation. I thought of how and why things had happened in the past. I thought of my eighty-year-old mum and of how rarely I saw her – even though she lived only twenty minutes away. It was always business first with me, and I began to feel guilty about that.

Outside, in Jo's garden, I teamed up with twenty-eight-year-old Lee Sanger and we set about tidying up the mess and restoring a bit of order. Lee was a volunteer and seemed a nice guy, but I was surprised when I learned that he was ex-army. We also shared a passion for flying. When Lee told me he dreamed of gaining his pilot's licence, I had to bite my tongue and keep silent about how I already had mine. He told me he had been with the Duke of Lancaster Regiment in Iraq but had been kicked out after coming down with post-traumatic stress disorder. He was still haunted by crippling flashbacks relating to his experiences in Iraq. Certain noises and smells transported him straight back to scenes of gunfire and death. Then he admitted he frequently felt suicidal and had actually tried to kill himself. Thoughts of Ernie and of my own dark times after the Falklands came flooding back. I was furious that Lee and other young men were still going through all this crap and were being treated so badly.

I'd felt the pressure building up in me for days, so I suppose I should not have been surprised by what happened next. But I was caught completely unawares when I suddenly broke down in tears. Tony – the tough guy – was crying like a baby in front of the cameras, and millions of viewers would be watching in a few weeks' time. It was embarrassing, but I did not care. I had reached a watershed in my life. Having seen the show, Mum told me later that it was the first time she had seen me cry since I was a little boy. I had seen mates burned and blown to pieces in the Falklands. I had lost my best mate in the Foreign Legion. I had buried my father and my two brothers. But I had never shed a tear during all that time. Now I could not stop! I was finally releasing everything that had built up in my subconscious over the previous twenty-seven years. I was overwhelmed by pent-up feelings about the futility and stupidity of war and yet more wasted lives.

At the end of the programme, I revealed my identity to Dave Kelly. He was overjoyed when I gave him a donation for DAISY UK and a smaller amount for himself and his wife, so they could go away on a well-deserved holiday. I also made a donation of twenty thousand pounds to Helping Hands and paid to have Jo's garden landscaped so that it looked really beautiful. I gave Lee three thousand pounds so that he might pursue his dream of taking flying lessons, and then offered to donate thirty thousand to the charity of his choice. He plumped for Combat Stress, so I decided to find out more about the organisation. What I discovered was a real eye-opener.

Combat Stress made me realise that almost *everyone* who takes part in a conflict is affected by it in some way, shape or form. I am not suggesting that all returning service personnel will suffer from clinical depression or develop full-blown post-traumatic stress disorder. But only nutcases can fail to be affected by their wartime experiences. The more I learned about PTSD, the more my own experiences started to make sense. The people at Combat Stress told me about the symptoms of the disorder – including emotional shut-down, anger, insularity, relationship difficulties and alcohol abuse – all of which sounded horribly familiar. I remembered all of those nights when I was angry and anxious, getting pissed and fighting people in pubs, or sitting at home depressed, not wanting to see anybody, drinking two bottles of wine and listening to music on my own until 4 a.m. I had been in distress and had not known it. I had been lucky to escape full-blown PTSD, but I was certainly still worried about things that had happened in the past – things I had tried to suppress.

Soon I would realise just how lucky I had been. I was shocked to learn that three hundred British Falklands veterans have committed suicide since returning from the South Atlantic, including thirty-seven paras. That is more than the 255 guys we lost while we were fighting down there. These were anguished souls who felt they had no option but to take their own lives. And they often did so in dramatic ways, as if they were making a protest or trying to get across a point. A former 2 Para sergeant who was at Goose Green died an agonising and horrific death after he handcuffed himself to the steering wheel of his car, doused himself with petrol and set himself on fire. Charles 'Nish' Bruce, a tough former para who served in the Falklands with the SAS, threw himself out of a light aircraft over

Oxfordshire without a parachute. A Welsh Guardsman who survived the *Sir Galahad* inferno hanged himself in his father's house on Remembrance Day. He symbolically timed his death for the eleventh hour of the eleventh day of the eleventh month.

If these dramatic acts of self-destruction were not screams for help, what was? These were big, hard, tough men, but they had been trained to kill, not to cope with death, destruction, disability and distress.

In addition to the suicides, the South Atlantic Medal Association (SAMA), a group that represents the interests of all Falklands veterans, estimates that around 2700 of the 30,000 personnel who served in the conflict have suffered from PTSD. Royal Navy veteran William Sutherland is one of SAMA's leading activists and I was aghast to hear of the devastating impact the war had wrought on his life. It had taken him to the very brink of suicide. He told me:

I actually put the barrel of my weapon into my mouth to get used to the taste of it. I had hit a brick wall and simply could not take any more. The flashbacks were like a horrible video playing over and over on a loop in my head. I just wanted to escape those horrible images. The only thing that stopped me was that I was worried about the effect it would have on one of the young lads finding me.

William still sported the trademark naval beard that he had grown during a twenty-one-year career which had taken him from being a teenager in Caithness in the north of Scotland to a highly skilled weapons expert with the rank of petty officer. He was intelligent, sensible and eloquent as we chatted over coffee in an Edinburgh hotel – a very together kind of guy, not the sort of bloke you would think had contemplated suicide.

William had been one of the sitting ducks we had watched being bombed in San Carlos Bay. He remembered:

I was a twenty-four-year-old leading seaman and artificer, a weapons expert, on HMS *Plymouth* when Argentina invaded. I actually had family in the Falklands and knew where they were. When it all kicked off on 2 April there were only two of us in the mess who even knew where the Falklands were.

We were among the first ships to sail and helped to recapture South Georgia when we fired 166 rounds of 4.5-inch high-explosive shells in three hours. The Argentine submarine *Santa Fe* was trapped there. It had been on the surface and one of our helicopters had put an anti-submarine missile through it so it couldn't dive. We asked them if they'd care to surrender and they kept saying 'no', so we kept throwing shells at them and eventually they said they would, so we had to take the POWs on board. Then we learned that the *Belgrano* was zigzagging its way in our direction and its big guns were bigger than our big guns, so we got out of there pretty fast.

Our next job was to lead the task force into San Carlos to establish the beachhead. The air raids started pretty soon after the troops landed. It was terrifying. We felt so exposed in that bay. Ships around us were bombed but we were lucky and emerged unscathed. HMS *Argonaut* was hit and sustained heavy damage. We rescued her at night as she had lost all her power. It looked like a scene from the Second World War. Men were clambering around the wreckage with torches. There were two fatalities on board. We buried them at sea. That's when the conflict became real to me. It's a moment that will stay with me for ever.

William's war got worse – a lot worse – when five Israeli-built Dagger jets flown by some of Argentina's best pilots sought out the *Plymouth*. He recalled:

On 8 June we got hit ourselves. People were scared. Nothing focuses the mind like being shot at. We had been tasked to do a daylight bombardment on West Falkland. Out of the blue, the alarm went off for Air Raid Warning

Red and we started firing the guns and missiles. We did the equivalent of a handbrake turn in a 2500-tonne warship to get back into San Carlos as quickly as possible. When the bombs hit, a massive depth charge – stored on the flight deck – came flying out and missed my head by a matter of inches. It easily could have exploded. I just nudged it overboard into the water.

I was lying on the deck, as was everyone who wasn't firing at the enemy, and I remember looking around me and seeing the sonar operators bouncing into the air each time we were hit. From my perspective, I felt as if everyone apart from me was bouncing into the air, but afterwards I was told I was as well. It was extremely terrifying – grown men were trying to crawl into the smallest places possible during very close calls. There were moments when I thought I was going to die. People were shouting because they were injured. It was a nightmare. There were terrible scenes – one of the guys had a twelve-inch piece of jagged red-hot steel sticking out of his head. It was the sort of thing you never forget.

Suddenly, something didn't sound right. Then my boss told me there was a raging inferno under a torpedo magazine. We had to go in and take the bottom layer of weapons out before they got too warm. We didn't want them going off. We managed to limp back to San Carlos.

Helicopters came out with specialist fire-fighting teams and a brain surgeon to treat the guy with the shrapnel sticking out of the top of his head.

The night of the surrender, we were sitting outside Stanley, ready to pound it to pieces. We were right where HMS *Glamorgan* had been the night before when it had been hit by an Exocet missile and thirteen men were killed. When the news came that it was all over, I was in my action station position and all I can remember is sliding down on to the deck off my chair with sheer exhaustion and relief.

But the war had taken its toll on the quietly spoken young sailor:

I wasn't the same man after I returned from the Falklands. Things like fire alarms or car alarms going off would wreck me. I used to enjoy going to the theatre, the cinema and concerts. But all of a sudden, within twenty minutes, I'd be soaked in cold sweat and I'd have to leave. The dimming of the theatre lights was enough to trigger a panic attack. At first I couldn't think why, but then it dawned on me. When you are doing the job on board ship, you turn down all the overhead lighting so that the computer and radar displays all stand out. The dimming lights were taking me back to those days of unbelievable, crackling tension in the South Atlantic.

I somehow continued to function and do my job, but it just got worse and worse until eventually I blew. One day, the first lieutenant asked me to take some new lads below deck for a firing exercise. I burst out crying – just broke down. I couldn't face another firing exercise. I was the duty officer for the ship that day, but the first lieutenant took the keys off me on the grounds of safety. I went to the sick bay and was put on sick leave. Eventually, I was discharged.

That was the end of William's naval career and the start of his lengthy battle with PTSD. It would prove to be a long, hard fight, with one of its consequences the disintegration of his marriage. For William, PTSD manifested itself in the constant strain of feeling that he could be killed at any moment – just as he had experienced when the *Plymouth* had come under attack. But there were many different types of stress.

Before leaving for the South Atlantic, Tony Davies, a tough regimental sergeant major with the Welsh Guards, was confident that he was ready for any challenges that the Falklands War might throw at him. But the stark reality of the war hit him almost immediately. He told me:

Defence Secretary John Nott confirms that our troops are firmly established after a day of fighting, 21 May. (Press Association)

We felt so sorry for the navy guys down in the bay below us. They were sitting ducks. HMS *Antelope* was sunk 23–24 May 1982. It was a terrible sight. (Press Association)

A grainy picture taken during a break in the fighting on the Falklands. I am wearing a woollen hat standing in the centre. Wayne Rees is to my right. Our faces are camouflaged for night fighting. (Tony Banks)

The Argentine garrison at Goose Green was much bigger than our intelligence suggested. Here we see surrendered weapons 28–29 May 1982. (Tony Banks)

The Argentines outnumbered us three to one. We could not believe there were so many prisoners taken at Goose Green. (Tony Banks)

Our commanding officer Lieutentant Colonel Herbert Jones was killed at Goose Green and awarded a posthumous VC but many of us felt that he had exposed himself to enemy fire unnecessarily and had been foolhardy. (Press Association)

A lot of the Argentinian conscripts were glad it was all over. They had been ill fed and poorly treated by their officers. Here a group is marched from Goose Green. (Press Association)

We could not believe that the *Sir Galahad* was sitting below us at Bluff Cove with the Welsh Guards still aboard. It was a disaster waiting to happen. Forty-eight soldiers and seamen died in our biggest setback of the war on 8 June 1982. (Press Association)

We saw terrible sights. Men were in agony from dreadful burns. We did what we could for them. The smell of burning flesh and plastic stuck with me for months. Here injured soldiers are coming ashore just after the attack. (Press Association)

We were shocked at the state of Port Stanley when we entered. Tragically three British civillians were killed by naval shelling but it could have been worse. (Hex)

Victory is ours. A good job well done. The British flag is hoisted again in Port Stanley. (Rex)

My war trophy was a regimental trumpet. I longed to know what had happened to the trumpeter. (Tony Banks)

Return to the Falklands. Going back to the Falklands with Jim Foster (left) and Wayne Rees (right) was a cathartic experience for me. Where I once fought, I now found inner peace. (Tony Banks)

Meeting Omar Tabarez at his home near Buenos Aires. He is a fine man and proud Argentine patriot. Like so many of us he had suffered from Combat Stress after the war. (Tony Banks)

With Omar and his two sons. (Tony Banks)

I was sixteen when I joined the Welsh Guards, so by the time I fought in the Falklands I was thirty-five and the regimental sergeant major. I was sort of a father figure for the regiment. We landed in the Falklands on 2 June and took over from 2 Para after Goose Green. We went to Fitzroy and Bluff Cove and we saw thirty-four men killed on the *Sir Galahad*. It's very hard to lose people. The Welsh regiments are like the Scottish regiments – you know a lot of the families. I had previously served with five of the guys who were killed. I knew a lot of their parents because of the closeness of the villages in Wales.

I had done five tours of Northern Ireland before the Falklands and I had seen guys killed there and bombs going off in Belfast. I had also done a year in Aden. Because I was the father of the regiment, I felt I was reasonably experienced and prepared for action. But when something like that happens, when *thirty-four* guys are killed, it's something you can never get used to. We saw guys with really horrendous injuries – lots of really badly burned bodies. It's something nobody can ever get over.

It was my regiment that was bombed on the *Sir Galahad* but I was lucky. Myself and a handful of others had arrived earlier. We had been ashore already for two days or it could have been us. On 8 June – a lovely, sunny day two ships docked at Fitzroy and they were bombed by the Argentinian Air Force. I was flown in by helicopter and there were lifeboats coming ashore with some horrendously injured people. They were in some sad states. Having said that, the guys really got things going despite what was going on around them. There were people helping inject morphine into others and helping them on to helicopters so they could get them to the SS *Uganda*, a hospital ship fifty miles off shore. Some were really badly wounded. It's really hard when anything kicks off, but when the ship was bombed we got an instant reaction – everybody was doing whatever they could for everyone else.

There were still more air raids coming – five that afternoon, in total – as guys were coming ashore. We were still having to deal with that as we tried to do our best for the guys. I was immensely proud of what these guys were doing for their friends. They were hearing people screaming in agony and seeing really badly burned bodies. I take my hat off to those kids – they were bloody brilliant! When the last of the air raids had finished and all the badly wounded had been flown back and you had the chance to sit down and think about it, that's when it started to become really difficult. We were thrown right back into the thick of it so it didn't give us time to dwell on it, even though we knew we had lost a lot of friends.

It still affects me today. I still remember lots of guys who were killed. I've met their mothers and fathers and, in some cases, I'm involved with their children. After the war, I had trouble sleeping. And I had a lot of flashbacks. I think most people did. I think I handled it myself – I drank a lot. If it got too much, I had time on my own. I had my own memories of what happened and I cooped it up. I bottled it up and got on with it. But, for some people, the cork just blows and they need treatment from places like Combat Stress.

I think the Falklands was the last honourable war that this country ever fought. I'm not taking anything away from the guys currently fighting in Afghanistan or those who did something similar in Iraq. But there were five thousand of us and we were ashore with no more supplies or reinforcements. It was the last proper war – the last all-out war. Every war involves people being killed, tragically. But, in Afghanistan, you hear of one guy being killed by an explosive device, or one guy getting shot. They are just taking one guy out here and there on a daily basis. But we were losing ten or fifteen guys a night. That's why some men are suffering from post-traumatic stress disorder. There were five thousand of us fighting shoulder to shoulder. Nothing like it has been fought since. And I don't think there will be anything quite like it again.

British soldiers look after each other. We all look after somebody who can't keep up, somebody who can't take as much as we can. But when you leave the services, you are more or less on your own. That's what a lot of guys can't handle. There is nobody to pick them up and look after them; nobody to steer them in the right direction.

I handled my problems, but some guys have committed suicide. They just don't know where to go, or who to see. It's difficult. There are organisations which are very good at handling these situations and looking out for the guys who are having problems. But so many guys leave the services and go out in the big, wide world that it's impossible to cover them all. There were twenty-nine thousand men in the Falklands War. The organisations are out there but, for some guys – tragically – it's just a little bit too late.

You don't really deal with it until the war is over. When you go back home and see the families, that's very hard. After the war had finished, we flew to Ascension Island then back to the RAF base at Norton. All the families and friends – and the families of some of the men who had been killed – met us when we came back. That was a really, really difficult time. They all came up and hugged us at the airport and there were lots of tears – including from me. It's one of those difficult times where you don't know what to

say and what not to say. I went around with the commanding officer visiting every single bereaved family after
that – it took us two or three weeks. That gave them some
sort of closure.

As veterans like William and Tony told me more and more
about PTSD, I started to appreciate the crucial work that
Combat Stress was doing. Commodore Andrew Cameron,
chief executive of the organisation, told me:

There has been a significant fall-out from the Falklands.
There were quite a few people who went down there not
knowing what they were going to get into. When the fleet
sailed from Portsmouth, there was quite a lot of concern.
People like Sandy Woodward, who was Taskforce
Commander, wrote in his book that he didn't think the
occupants of the ships on the way down really thought they
were going to fight. Then they got to the South Atlantic,
which is a highly isolated, extremely forbidding place. It is
cold, very windy and the weather changes rapidly. It is quite
disconcertingly disorientating. It is very wet and all of a
sudden, as a soldier, you are landed on a beach in the
middle of nowhere, to fight an enemy who you never
thought you would be fighting, because three months
before they were your mates. Half the stuff you need to go

to war with is not there because it's been sunk, including helicopters. There is no clear war plan because the only place you could take is Port Stanley and you're on the other side of the island. There was a lot of political oversight trying to drive things, so there was a huge amount of confusion. It was a chamber of horrors in a very cold, wet environment, even before the fighting began. For the first time, you had people scattering anti-personnel mines out the back of helicopters, so you didn't have marked minefields, and people were having their feet blown off by things that couldn't be found with metal detectors. All in all, it was very short and very nasty.

I recognised Andrew's picture of the Falklands War all right, but I was shocked to learn of the scale of PTSD among the veterans. I was also surprised to learn that the average time it takes for the condition to be diagnosed is around thirteen years. Thankfully, that time is decreasing because people are beginning to talk about it. PTSD is no longer the condition that dare not speak its name, and the days of the stiff upper lip are drawing to an end. Captain David Hart-Dyke, the father of comedian Miranda Hart, has recently admitted that he was unable to talk about his experiences in the Falklands for years. (He commanded HMS *Coventry* on a daring decoy mission to lure the Argies away from San Carlos Bay, but the ship was attacked by Argie Skyhawks and sank with the loss of nineteen men. Hart-Dyke himself was badly burned in the incident.) Meanwhile, Ken Lukowiak, an old comrade from 2 Para, has written a best-selling book in which he describes his PTSD and admits that he still suffers flare-ups every year between April and June.

The stigma relating to PTSD may be diminishing, but it still takes a lot of courage to talk about it, not least because of the continuing peer pressure to be manly and bottle things up. Another veteran who has bravely spoken out is Les Standish, a former corporal with 2 Para and a leading figure in SAMA. Les was a combat medical technician, attached to 2 Field Hospital, and was aboard the *Sir Galahad* when it was hit. He told the *Daily Mail* that he was on the tank deck when the air strike hit and luckily was protected from the explosion. He soon appreciated the reality of the situation. He gathered a group of medics and began helping the wounded. As the smoke began to clear Les realised the fire was spreading. He noticed a pile of munitions in the centre of the deck. 'Basically a giant bomb waiting to explode!'

As they moved forward to evacuate the casualties, Les saw a soldier waving his arms for help. The man had been disembowelled and his leg had been partially amputated and Les knew he was beyond help. 'I had to make a decision and I left him,' Les said. 'I've felt guilt and regret for twenty-five years that I didn't even say anything to him.'

As Les came to the bottom of a stairwell he saw two young Welsh Guardsmen who were also in a bad way. 'They shook each other's hands, pointed their rifles to each other's head and pulled their triggers ... When I thought back to this incident I just felt so disgusted with myself – that I had felt no sympathy, remorse or other emotion.'

Les eventually got his casualty out and went on with his job, before being casevaced ashore and re-kitted. He spent the rest of the war in Fitzroy working with the surgical team.

Les has been through the torments of hell with PTSD and has done a lot to highlight just how pernicious the disorder can be. It is all the more insidious for being invisible – psychological rather than physical.

Former Welsh Guardsman Chris Duggan was also traumatised by the bombing of the *Sir Galahad*. His campaign for PTSD sufferers was recognised with a Speaking Out Award at the Mental Health Media Awards. He vividly recalls the smell of his injured comrades as a cross between 'burned pork and plastic', adding, 'I can still taste it.' It was eight years before his condition was identified, and during that time his marriage disintegrated and he nearly died.

Chris joined the army as a boy soldier at the age of sixteen and he had served in Northern Ireland and Cyprus before the

Falklands, but nothing prepared him for what unfolded on 8 June 1982, when the *Sir Galahad* was hit. In an interview with the *Guardian* he recalled:

> We were on a 'foraging' expedition, scrounging some fags and booze for our boys. We heard 'all hands' and we went up to the field hospital. These helicopters were coming in and we were asked to help get the boys off. We didn't know who they were or what had happened, but when they opened the doors the stench was horrendous.

Chris makes a telling point about the impact of the attack, in which forty-eight men lost their lives: 'In Northern Ireland, we had deaths. But it was one at a time. It was terrible, but you could handle it. But these were very close friends of mine, many I had known since 1970.'

Later, Chris was ordered to sort through the dead men's kit so that personal effects and clothing could be returned to their families. Within weeks, he was back in England on leave. There was no counselling, nor even a debriefing. He claims that a new commander of the Welsh Guards told the men simply to 'forget the Falklands'.

It was little wonder that his world collapsed when he left the army in 1986. Chris suffered many of the classic symptoms of PTSD:

I was verbally aggressive, very uncooperative. I was arguing with the wife, and eventually we divorced. I decided to change the kitchen around one day and get all new stuff. I threw everything out of the window. I was ten storeys up in a flat. I poured brandy all over the video and it melted. I flooded the bathroom.

Chris's neighbour took him to a doctor who prescribed antidepressants. When Chris did not take them he suffered uncontrollable bouts of crying, violent outbursts and hallucinations. He was haunted by visions of people who had died on the ship and would see them driving a milkfloat or in the faces of policemen. He was eventually hospitalised and prescribed a cocktail of tranquillisers and antidepressants, but still nobody linked his condition with his military service. Chris only heard about PTSD after meeting an army mate who was also suffering from the disorder and put him in touch with his psychiatrist: 'He told me I should see his doctor – Jonathan Bisson, a consultant psychiatrist at University Hospital, Cardiff, and a specialist in PTSD. He recognised PTSD straight away.' That illustrates just how hit-and-miss diagnosis was in the thirty years after the Falklands.

Bisson referred Chris to Combat Stress, and he is now a staunch supporter of the charity. He feels it should be running the armed forces' mental health services, describing the NHS as 'too clinical' and the Ministry of Defence as 'too authoritarian' for the task.

As I thought about PTSD, I remembered returning from the Falklands and the army sending us all to see psychiatrists, who concluded that something like 70 per cent of us were mentally ill. But the whole process was not taken seriously and I know some guys just made up stuff during the interviews. In any event, there was no mechanism in place to look out for us afterwards. Of course, I heard stories of guys going off the rails, but I did not connect their experiences with the Falklands or realise that PTSD could take so long to develop. The army is much wiser to the condition now, and senior NCOs and officers all receive training in spotting PTSD. However, there is still a stigma attached to it. People fear that if they put their hand up and say, 'Yep, I'm suffering from depression,' it will affect their career. So they tend to keep quiet and carry on. This is a major problem for the military. Tens of thousands of pounds are invested in training our soldiers, so, in purely economic terms, surely it would be better to try to fix the guys who suffer from PTSD, rather than discard them. And that would certainly be the right thing to do morally. For a guy like Lee Sanger, the army was his life. He was so distraught when he was forced out that he tried to kill himself. That cannot be right.

As I learned more about PTSD, one awful thought that

struck me was that if all of the Falklands veterans are only coming to the fore now, what on earth is it going to be like in a few years' time? Britain has been involved in conflicts almost continuously since 1991 – in the first Gulf War, the Balkans, Sierra Leone, Iraq and Afghanistan. So it seems likely that there will soon be an epidemic of armed forces mental health problems. Combat Stress estimates that 45,000 of the 180,000 British military personnel who have served in Iraq and Afghanistan to date will have mental health issues, and 9000 will develop full-blown PTSD.

The *Secret Millionaire* programme showed me that I was in a privileged position and had the capacity to help people. It got me thinking that I should use my profile to champion the causes I believe in – and that is what I have tried to do. Previously, I had never really seen myself as a millionaire, because I had always been working. If you have money, you can buy a bigger house, a better car and longer holidays, but you will not necessarily find happiness. That comes from within.

So I was pleased to get involved with Combat Stress and its 'Enemy Within' Appeal, which aimed to raise thirty million pounds to meet the growing challenge of PTSD in ex-service personnel. The main problem we have is that the public is fickle. Help for Heroes has done a fantastic job, raising almost a hundred million pounds in just three years. It has captured the public's imagination and has also been a great supporter of Combat Stress. Since it came on the scene, donations to all military charities have increased significantly. However, my fear is that when the boys finally come home from Afghanistan and the next disaster comes along – be it a tsunami or an earthquake – everyone will forget about the military charities. So they have to raise as much money as possible in this brief window of opportunity.

Secret Millionaire also made me reassess the Falklands War and wonder whether it had all been worthwhile. I had just been a young laddie at the time of the fighting, and ever since I had tried to bury such thoughts. Now, though, I wanted to take a fresh look at the conflict.

And there was a personal connection that had always intrigued me. I had taken quite a few battlefield souvenirs – cap badges, bayonets, compasses and berets. But over the years I had given them all away. The only one I had kept was the shiny black box containing the regimental trumpet and the little book with the Argie soldier's name. Who was Omar Rene Tabarez? I could imagine this guy, nineteen or twenty years old, writing his music with his own hand in the barracks and dreaming of being a musician. What had happened to him? Was he still alive? Had he prospered and had a family? Had he suffered from PTSD? How did he feel about the Falklands?

I decided to track him down and – if he was still alive – reunite him with his trumpet. I would also return to the Falklands – to San Carlos Bay, Goose Green, Wireless Ridge and Port Stanley – and try to lay the ghosts of the Falklands to rest.

CHAPTER 7

CRY FOR ARGENTINA

Meeting Lee Sanger on *Secret Millionaire* and learning about PTSD made me realise what a massive influence the Falklands War had had on my life. Yet, for nearly thirty years, I had tried to minimise and forget the whole experience. Now, though, I thought that if I could learn more about the war, track down Omar Tabarez and return his trumpet, I might be able to conclude a chapter in my life, and move on. The overwhelming anger I had felt towards the Argentinian soldiers after their surrender had long subsided. I now appreciated that the regular soldiers had only been doing their job – just like us – while the bedraggled conscripts had found themselves on the receiving end of night attacks and bombardments by one of the world's best-trained armies. We had all been victims of the politicians' failures.

The trumpet did not belong to me and I wanted to hand it back. But that was not going to be easy. I mulled over how to return it for months. How would I find its owner? And, if he was still alive, what kind of reception would I receive? He might slam the door in my face. The issue of the Falklands/Malvinas was still rumbling along, with the UK and Argentina at loggerheads over the ownership of the islands, especially now that drilling for oil was under way.

I was undeterred, though, and after an exhaustive trawl of the internet I found an Irish freelance journalist called Jeff Farrell who accepted a commission to locate Omar. Coincidentally, I attended a business lunch in Glasgow where I met Atholl Duncan, the head of news and current affairs at BBC Scotland, who had seen and enjoyed the *Secret Millionaire* programme. When I told him the story of the trumpet he was thrilled and said it would make a good human-interest documentary. He suggested that BBC Scotland could film the whole trip, and I was happy to agree.

Eventually, after months of searching, Jeff Farrell got in touch. Apparently, Omar was alive and well. He was now a history teacher and lived with his wife, also a teacher, and their two sons in a little town near Buenos Aires. Jeff had contacted him through an army veterans' organisation and told me that

Omar was amenable to meeting up. He was particularly looking forward to getting his trumpet back. Nearly three decades after the liberation of Port Stanley, it seemed that we would meet again.

I was still a little apprehensive about the trip to Argentina. There was speculation in the Scottish media that I might be arrested for stealing the trumpet, and I could not imagine that a 2 Para veteran would be the most popular visitor to Buenos Aires.

Driving into the capital from the airport was like driving into Milan. The whole feel of the place was very cosmopolitan and European. The city abounded with monuments, statues and parks between the impressive buildings. The Porteños, as the locals are known, are busy, big-city types – brusque and to the point. It was not long before I spotted 'Malvinas' bumper-stickers, window posters, flags and the occasional bit of graffiti. The man from the British Embassy filled me in on the current situation and I began to realise just how much the Falklands/Malvinas mean to ordinary Argentinians. To them, the Malvinas are as Argentinian as the tango, Eva Perón and Maradona. Reclaiming the islands from the British is enshrined as a goal of Argentina's constitution, and schoolchildren have been taught of the supposed injustice of British rule for generations. In the famous Plaza de Mayo in front of the pink Casa Rosada presidential palace –

where the white-headscarved mothers of the disappeared victims of the Dirty War parade each week – a permanent camp of Malvinas logistics veterans was demanding pensions but also the return of the islands. Every town in the country has a monument, street or plaza dedicated to the Malvinas. However, on a personal level, I encountered no ill-feeling or enmity.

After doing some filming in Buenos Aires, I got a bit of time off and went to see Scotland playing rugby in Tucumán, in the north of the country. We were the first team to beat Argentina twice in tests in their own country – not even the All Blacks have managed that feat. The stadium was absolutely jammed – packed to its 32,000 capacity. There were hardly any Scots there, of course, but there was a great atmosphere. And then we won! The few of us who had made the trip got to meet the team afterwards. It was just great. I chatted with BBC Scotland's Jim Mason, who described Tucumán as 'a rugby region, Argentina's equivalent of the Borders'. The locals looked like Andean Indians. They were indigenous natives, not like the European-looking population of Buenos Aires, and really friendly. Even the police wanted their photographs taken with us.

Finally the day came when I was due to meet Omar Tabarez and return his trumpet. We drove for about an hour and a half out of Buenos Aires, into the countryside. By now, I was really anxious about how it would go. Maybe, like me, he had lost pals in the war. Maybe he was an Argentinian nationalist, a fanatic. Maybe he had suffered from PTSD. As we walked up the garden path to his small bungalow, my heart was racing. I did not know what to expect.

When the door opened, I saw that the house was full of people. Every man and his dog seemed to be there. That took me by surprise. Grannies, aunties, uncles, brothers and kids had all turned up. I handed Omar the trumpet and instinctively we hugged. His mother and wife became very emotional at that point. They were chatting away excitedly and the interpreter told me, 'This means a great deal to them.' It was a very moving moment. I was choking back the tears. On his doorstep, Omar was very formal and proper. In front of the cameras, he made a very statesmanlike little speech about the historic importance of the moment. He could have been a diplomat. Standing on the doorstep, he told me:

This act shows you're a man of deep honour. There is no price for this act of kindness. I really appreciate this. I always dreamed of getting my trumpet back. It gives me comfort. It is like getting a brother back. You are very brave to come here to Argentina and do this and to return something that belongs to a soldier. You didn't take the decision to confront me – Maggie Thatcher did. It was a job we had to do. We were soldiers sent there, and only boys acting as men. The politicians and the governments, they sent us there, not us.

He added that he had been 'jumping for joy' since a former army colleague had phoned him to say I wanted to reunite him with the instrument. 'I could not believe it,' he said. 'I am still only putting my feet back on the ground. It has a lot of meaning for me. It's symbolic. It's like therapy. My trumpet accompanied me through the war. It was like my brother.'

When we entered the compact house, Omar welcomed us warmly, saying that his home was small but his heart was large. And so it proved to be. As we sat down, he began to relax and told me his story.

He was one of a family of six from the Entre Rios Province in the north-east of Argentina. His father had worked in a meat refrigeration plant but there were few employment opportunities for a working-class boy in the 1970s. Like most Argentinian kids, the young Omar was football daft, but he was also interested in music and joined a band that was started by the parish priest. After he displayed some talent, the priest arranged for him to join the musical branch of the army as a boy soldier. That was in 1977, when Omar was just fifteen. The murderous Dirty

War, conducted by the army against left-wing opponents, was at its height at the time, but young Omar was simply grateful for a job and a chance to hone his musical talents. I had the impression that he stayed out of politics and kept his nose clean.

In 1982, their officers got Omar and his mates together and told them they were off to reclaim the Malvinas. Omar recalled that they all felt a terrific surge of national pride when they heard the announcement. Like all Argentinians, he had been taught the injustice of the British occupation of the Malvinas ever since primary school, where it was included in history and geography lessons. He had flown in as part of the garrison reinforcements to Port Stanley, which they had renamed Puerto Argentina, on 2 April – the very first day of the invasion. At that point, most of the young Argies were a bit like us – they never really thought it would come to a full-on shooting war. The fascist junta was banking on their pals in the Reagan administration to back them up and force the British government to the negotiating table. But they had not reckoned on Maggie Thatcher.

Omar had an important ceremonial duty to perform: each morning, he sounded his trumpet as Argentina's national flag was raised over the islands. He had a military role to play too, of course: he was attached to an artillery detachment defending the vital airport at Port Stanley. The Argentinian officers kept their troops in the dark about a lot of things. For instance, Omar was never told that the *Belgrano* had been sunk or that the Argentinian Navy had been effectively knocked out of the war. Instead, he and his comrades were fed propaganda to the effect that the *Canberra* – the main British troopship – had been sunk, with tremendous loss of life. The conscripts, in particular, were bored, cold and poorly fed. At first, they received well-wishing letters from schoolchildren and morale-boosting messages from home, but these dried up as the British blockade of the islands tightened. Despite the propaganda, both regulars and conscripts became prey to terrifying rumours, many of which related to the ferocity of the Gurkhas and their legendary ability to decapitate foes with one swipe of the *kukri*. Nevertheless, Omar and his friends in the regular army still felt that they were doing their patriotic duty, and they were prepared to die to defend their nation.

During the defence of Port Stanley, Omar would witness one of the most amazing feats of airmanship in the history of warfare. At 4 a.m. on 1 May, a lone British Vulcan bomber suddenly appeared over the airport and dropped a stick of twenty-one thousand-pound bombs across the runway. In the longest bombing raid ever staged, Flight Lieutenant Martin Withers had refuelled several times in mid-air while covering the 7500 kilometres from Wideawake Airfield on Ascension Island. This daring mission took Argentina and the world by total surprise and earned Withers a Distinguished Flying Cross. Omar recalled:

I was sharing a dug-out at the end of the runway, close to a watch-tower. Our first bombing was terrifying – there was tremendous noise and the earth shook. Six of us scrambled out of the dug-out and took cover, shaking under some excavators that were scattered around the runway. We did not know what was happening or what to do. We decided to run for it – to our command post – to get instructions. But as we got out and dashed towards our command bunker, I realised that I had left the regimental flag and trumpet behind. I told the others to go ahead and then ran back to get the trumpet and the flag. There was chaos, bombing and fire all around. When I got to the command post, the officer in charge told me to sound the alarm with my trumpet. I blew the call to indicate that we were under attack as hard as I could. But it was difficult to compete with the explosions of thousand-pound bombs, and people later commented that it sounded surreal to hear the trumpet warning being sounded during the raid.

Omar had the misfortune to be based in the most shelled spot on the islands, and this baptism of fire was an indicator of awful things to come. Two of his fellow soldiers were killed in the raid and dozens wounded, and although the damage to the airfield was relatively slight and it was easily repaired, the attack was a shock for the defenders. In the weeks that followed, the airport was bombed from the air, shelled by land-based artillery and bombarded by ships of the Royal Navy. It was not a healthy place to be, and Omar was lucky to emerge physically unscathed. However, the extreme stress of being under sustained attack would have a devastating psychological impact on him.

I struggled to maintain my composure as the familiar story of PTSD – the story I had heard so often back in Britain – unfolded once again. As soon as he had opened the door, I had noticed that Omar was quite pale – much paler than in photos taken on the Falklands when, as a nineteen-year-old, he had posed with his trumpet and a captured Union Flag. In those pictures, he looked typically Latino and tanned; now, he looked more like a northern European. It transpired that he had lost the pigmentation of his skin as a result of a condition called vitiligo, induced by the stress of his wartime experiences. After leaving the army in 1995, he struggled to find his feet. He has suffered flashbacks and nightmares, and rarely spoke about the war before Jeff Farrell got in touch and told him about the plan to return the trumpet. During a thunderstorm in the 1990s, he pushed his infant son under the bed, convinced that they were being bombarded by artillery shells. He has also suffered from depression. His wife and family have been very supportive and Omar has been treated for his anxiety, but one especially disturbing dream still haunts him during times of stress. He explained, 'It is a terrible vision of zombie-like Argentinian soldiers, my comrades, coming down the bleak hillsides of the Falklands towards me with their arms outstretched, pleading for help, walking on bloody stumps that once were legs.'

Another flashback related to the day in May 1982 when he went to the cemetery in Port Stanley. He recalled, 'When I got there, I saw the bodies of my dead comrades inside white plastic bags. The blood of my dead comrades was coming out from those bags and was running on the ground. A British missile had targeted an Argentinian radar installation that was operated by four of my friends. Among them was a close friend called Dachary. It was a very hard moment for me because after seeing that terrible scene and impact, I had to play the one minute silence with my trumpet. The trumpet sounded loud but at the same time it sounded with pain and tears.'

My heart went out to Omar and tears came to my eyes as he told me how he had suffered since the war – like so many other veterans, both British and Argentinian. I admired and respected him. He had been prepared to die for the Malvinas and passionately believed in his country's cause. He eloquently summed up the experience of many veterans on both sides: 'The war did not stop in 1982. It goes on for life. It is an internal struggle and the suffering goes on.' I understood perfectly, because what Omar was saying chimed with my own experiences of life after the Falklands.

It makes me furious that so many veterans have had to endure the same mental trauma and that they have received so little help. Now, I wanted to meet some of Omar's comrades to hear their stories and discover how they had coped after the war. Omar was a gracious host and a few days later he arranged a real Argentinian barbecue out in the countryside. We drove for quite a distance to a place called Plomer. There was a tiny, picturesque former railway station, seemingly in the middle of nowhere, and opposite it a former social club/café built in the colonial style at the end of the nineteenth century. As I watched two grizzled gauchos organising the truly gigantic barbecue, I realised that this was the authentic rural Argentina.

Quite a few military types were there. All were veterans, former regulars in the army and navy, and friends of Omar. They were good blokes and seemed genuinely pleased to meet me. As the beef sizzled and the red wine flowed, I listened to their stories with interest and mounting sadness. Among them was Carlos Montiel, who had been a corporal in the 3rd Regiment of the Argentinian Army – the guys who had given 2 Para so much grief at Goose Green. Now a school caretaker, he had filled the cavernous interior of the social club with his huge collection of Argentinian and British books on the conflict. It seemed that his way of coping with the war had been to become an enthusiast for it, but as he earnestly showed me his library, it soon became clear that he had suffered from its legacy, too. He recalled the outbreak of war:

I was surprised to hear the news on 2 April that we were going to recover the islands. Of course, I felt great pride, as all Argentinians did. But as we flew into the Malvinas I never imagined that there would be a real war. We all just assumed that negotiations would resolve the issue peacefully. To begin with, I was stationed at the airport and the first air raid – on 1 May – was an awful experience. It came as a complete surprise. I saw terrible, unforgettable sights. Until then, we had not really thought about war; now, we were facing the reality. I was also under bombardment on Mount Challenger and Mount Kent. When the British attacked Darwin and Goose Green on 28 May we were flown up in helicopters as reinforcements for the 3rd Regiment, which was holding off your comrades in 2 Para. We landed shortly before nightfall behind our lines and had only gone about three hundred metres when there was a terrific explosion behind us. I looked around and the two helicopters that had brought us in were in flames. It was a terrifying close escape. Then we had to march four kilometres under constant shelling to our trenches. Several of my friends were wounded.

The British were attacking Darwin. We had some good positions that were well dug-in and the British scouts missed them. We were under constant attack from helicopters. There were always helicopters shooting at us and ships shelling us. I arrived at Darwin when it was almost at the point of surrender, but my regiment had held back the British and, of course, the British Colonel Jones who wanted war and behaved like he was crazy was killed. Mine was one of the two regiments that suffered the most – in which most soldiers died. Thirty-six soldiers in my regiment were killed.

Of course, unlike the British, the surviving Argie soldiers had then faced the indignity – and terror – of surrender. I learned that many of them were told by their officers and NCOs that they would be massacred by the British and their Gurkha mercenaries if they surrendered. Omar told me that one of his most terrifying moments came when he was being repatriated: 'We were on a ship taking us out to the main vessel that would bring us back. The guards had their guns trained on us when the side of the ship was dropped down. I thought, This is it. We are all going to be shot and thrown over the side. That is how anxious we were. We were so relieved when the British simply started throwing rubbish over the side.'

The memory of capture was still vivid for Carlos:

It was the saddest day of my life. It happened on 29 May, Argentina's national day for the army. But my regiment was the only one that surrendered with honour. The British honoured them. They said that they had to be honoured because of their bravery and courage when they fought. We were more or less well treated by the British. It was a delicate situation because while we were surrendering, there were other people who were still fighting on another part of the island.

We were taken to a place where sheep were kept. The British soldiers asked the Argentinian soldiers to move some ammunition supplies. We didn't know how it happened, but those supplies exploded and some of our soldiers were killed in the explosion. Some people said that the British killed those soldiers by placing something underneath to explode. We were alarmed and frightened and feared the worst. I saw a British soldier shoot an Argentinian prisoner who was really badly wounded. After the explosion, this soldier lost one foot and he was burned all over. He was shaking and screaming. So the British soldier shot him. We considered it a mercy action. I will never be able to forget that. I sometimes suffer from flashbacks. But I try to focus on my life because, if not, those flashbacks can make me feel very bad.

Omar told me that when he returned to the mainland he was greeted with a military band and given a hero's welcome. However, Carlos's return was very different and, I discovered, much more typical. To the embattled junta, the defeated troops were an embarrassing reminder of a failed gamble. To the public, they were a painful symbol of shameful national indignity. Young men who had risked their lives for their country were whisked away to barracks and told not to speak of the Malvinas. Many had to sign a declaration that they would remain silent. Incredibly, in the years to come, they were shunned by society and employers, with many suffering active discrimination. For years, penniless, unemployed veterans – who were also denied a state pension – were a regular sight on the Buenos Aires Metro, begging in order to raise money for wheelchairs or false limbs. These traumatised veterans, often from remote villages in distant parts of the country, were known as '*los pibes malvinas*' – the Malvinas boys. Prior to joining the army, many of them had never even seen the sea or snow. They had been plucked from the countryside for their one year of national service, given a smattering of military training and subjected to weeks of high-explosive terror. Then they had suffered humiliation at the hands of their enemies, followed by rejection by their own people. Inevitably, many slipped into mental health problems and alcohol and drug abuse. So many lives ruined because of a stupid gamble – it was heartbreaking.

Carlos remembered the bitter years after the war:

There was no welcome party for us. Quite the opposite. When I arrived in Buenos Aires, I was taken straight to an army school. I was not made welcome. When I finally got home and met my family, I was euphoric and could not stop talking. Then I fell asleep for three days. I found it very hard to readjust. I could not communicate well with other people. I had to leave the military because I used to argue with all my comrades. I was never offered help of any kind.

I had a lot of problems. I had marriage problems. I had three other girlfriends. I could not maintain a stable marriage. For twenty-two years, I never spoke about the Malvinas. Some relatives were even unaware that I was a veteran because I never spoke about the Malvinas after my homecoming. It was my new girlfriend, who is a teacher, who taught me that I had to talk about it. When I first started to speak to her about the Malvinas, I cried. I was able to describe my feelings for the first time.

After that, I started to buy books about the Malvinas and read about the conflict. Now I am able to speak about it and have built up my book collection as a sort of therapy. It has become a passion and has helped me. Some people criticise me because I have British books, but I think we need both sides of the story to learn how to arrange things to avoid a future war.

Omar and his comrades had been professional soldiers, so it was understandable that they were reluctant to criticise the Argentinian Army, especially when talking with an outsider. But as he relaxed, Omar hinted that some Argie soldiers had been badly treated during the war. He himself had been left to walk miles back to camp on his own after sounding the trumpet each morning while an officer drove back in a jeep. And, as hunger had set in, he and his mates had been forced to forage along the shoreline for shellfish. I knew that there was a fault-line dividing the Malvinas veterans. Some conscripts had started court proceedings against officers, alleging ill-treatment. Meanwhile, an award-winning film – *Illuminated by Fire* – based on a book by a former conscript, Edgardo Esteban, had provoked massive controversy. Esteban's house had even been bombed. I sensed that few of Omar's friends would have much sympathy for the conscripts' organisations that were linked to left-wing groups. One of them referred to Esteban, a respected television journalist, as 'a liar, a traitor and a coward'.

But I was not going to let politics spoil a good party. To the delight of all, Omar showed that he had not lost his touch with the trumpet. The sacred silver cornet was produced from its case and the regimental bugle calls that had summoned his comrades on the Malvinas now sounded out peacefully across the pampas as clear as a bell. While seemingly endless vast plates of meat were washed down with fine Argentine Malbec, I fell into conversation with Reinaldo Solizo, a burly naval veteran in his late fifties. He was a likeable man who became visibly moved as he recalled the friends he had lost when the *Belgrano* was sunk by HMS *Conqueror*. He had flown out to the Falklands to crew a small supply ship, one of four that shuttled men, food and ammunition to the army outposts that were dotted around the islands. Because he was a little older than many of the young soldiers, he became something of a father figure to them. He even had to show some of them how to use their weapons. His craggy features creased as he recalled:

I felt sorry for the young soldiers. It was true that they did not have enough food. They used to kill the lambs that were there and they used to eat the meat without salt. If they were stationed in isolated positions, they did not receive enough assistance. They did not even have enough clothes to keep themselves warm. There were days when it rained a lot and they got soaked. When the sun was shining, they used to take their clothes off to dry them and they used to work in their underwear, even though it was so cold in the Malvinas at that time.

We used to take the soldiers potatoes and beans. One soldier was so hungry that he boarded a ship to see if he could get something to eat and he almost got killed by the soldiers standing guard on the ship. That was at Port Howard, near San Carlos. The soldiers stationed at Port Howard mostly came from two provinces, Corrientes and Misiones, in the northern part of Argentina, and it is very hot there. These soldiers had been forced to leave behind everything they owned. They just had their backpacks, their guns and what they were wearing. That is why they suffered a lot from the cold, because they came straight from Misiones and Corrientes. The soldiers suffered from starvation because the operation was not well organised.

Reinaldo and his shipmates lived under the constant threat of attack as they sailed around the islands, hugging the rocky shoreline in case they had to swim for it. They watched land positions coming under bombardment, and eventually one ship in their small flotilla was sunk.

We were all worried that submarines would attack us. Some of us used to dream about submarines and see the British underneath the water, watching us from their periscopes. One of our ships was packed with munitions when it was attacked by a British ship. It was hit eight times and exploded. Two days later, we went back to the spot where the ship was sunk. We found bodies bobbing up and down in the sea and saw wreckage from the ship floating in the ocean. We took those bodies to Port Howard and buried them there. Among the dead were some civilian volunteers.

Amazingly, about a week after the sinking, two survivors were found alive. They had managed to swim to a small island where there was an abandoned house. It was a really small house but they found some milk and there were some sheep. They were so cold, they used the fleeces from the sheep to cover up and stay warm. When we found them, they looked like something from the Bronze Age. One was a naval captain and the other was a volunteer from Seville, in Spain. He had volunteered to cross the Atlantic to go to war. It was a terrifying period and we thought we could be attacked at any time.

Reinaldo was on the verge of tears several times as he spoke, and it was plain that he had been deeply affected by his experiences.

After the war, I continued working in the navy as an electrician, so I did not have a problem when it came to a job. But many returning soldiers, especially conscripts, had a lot of problems after the war. They could not find a job because people knew they were conscripts. They did not give them an opportunity because they said they had mental problems. Many of them could not find a job to survive.

It is very hard for me to talk about the Malvinas. I feel very sad and anxious when I think about it. I joined the navy with a lot of the crew of the *Belgrano*. When I remember my friends who died in the Malvinas conflict, I feel depressed. I feel much sorrow and pain when I go to the war memorial in Plaza San Martin and see their names. I feel such pain in my heart and I cannot find comfort.

Omar and his friends had given me such a heartfelt welcome, and after a rousing send-off I returned to Buenos Aires with a warm glow. Returning the trumpet had definitely been the right thing to do. At first, it had felt strange to be surrounded by guys who I had once tried to kill and who had killed some of my good mates. But we had a common bond of humanity and the unifying experience of the ordeal of war. The Malvinas still meant a great deal to them, and I mulled over the similarity and intensity of the post-war experiences suffered by veterans on both sides.

My visit to Argentina was a big news story in the country's media, and the army staged an impressive official trumpet handover ceremony in Buenos Aires. A whole battalion was there, with everyone in full regalia, as well as television cameras, generals and a priest. It was an amazing experience and obviously meant a lot to them. The officers clearly viewed my visit and the return of the trumpet as a private act between two soldiers. It was not a political thing at all. Major Dario Ochoa, who coordinated the ceremony, neatly summed it up when he told reporters: 'We, as soldiers, have more in common than governments. We understand each other. Mr Banks has a nice attitude towards this and the army is happy the veteran will get his trumpet back.'

But afterwards, we went to a military radio station, and they really tried to make a political deal of it all. As soon as I got a sense of that, I switched off. The odd veteran tried it on with me, and I just walked away from it. I always stuck to the same line: 'I have no animosity towards Argentina. I was sent to the Falklands to do a job and that was that. I am not here to change history. I just came here to return something that was not mine.'

On one occasion, we went to a mock-Falklands cemetery that had been carefully constructed as a memorial to the Argentinian fallen. It even had a small church. I walked among the crosses and looked at the names of the boys who had died. There were the expected Spanish names but also a lot of English-, Welsh- and Scottish-sounding names – descendants of migrants who had travelled to Argentina in the nineteenth century. Seeing those names really brought it home to me that these poor lads really had been just like me. We were all just soldiers doing what we were paid for. I met some veterans there, including a pilot who tried to get political with me, but I refused to take him on. Another veteran spoke really good English, and claimed to have been involved in negotiations between Britain and Argentina over the future of the islands. He maintained that a deal was almost done to fly three flags over the Falklands/Malvinas. The idea was that the flags of Britain, Argentina and an independent Falklands would flutter above Port Stanley. But it fell through at the last moment.

Meeting Omar and his mates was a cathartic – and profoundly moving – experience for me. But I felt that there was still more to learn. I wanted to hear the 'unofficial' side of the story – how the conscripts had fared during and after the war. I was shocked by what I discovered.

First, I learned the full, appalling story of the hundreds of Argentinian veterans, both regulars and conscripts, who had committed suicide since the end of the war. The rate peaked at around fifty a year in 2000 – once again demonstrating the time-lag between horrific events and the onset and development of PTSD. As in Britain, some of those who took their own lives chose to do so in the most dramatic way imaginable, probably to draw attention to their own and their comrades' suffering. The case of Corporal Eduardo Paz, a gunner who served in the Argentinian Navy, had similar symbolism to the death of the Welsh Guardsman who hanged himself at 11 a.m. on 11 November. Eduardo left his home in the city of Rosario on the night of 22 November 1999 and went to the 210-feet-high Monument to the National Flag that dominates the town. He spent hours filing through the railings to gain access to the monument. Then, when he finally reached the top of the hallowed tower, Eduardo jumped. He was thirty-eight years old and left behind six children. The dramatic nature of his self-sacrifice focused some attention on the veterans, but the sad fact is that men had been dying long before his suicide and they continued to do so afterwards.

Another naval veteran, Romualdo Bazan, was a bona fide hero. When his ship was attacked, Romualdo, who couldn't swim, plunged into the sea to rescue a comrade. He received the Argentinian Medal for Courage, joined the police force, and was eventually promoted to sergeant. But he was still haunted by the war, and in 2006 he hanged himself in his own home, leaving behind two children. Juan Loncopán, a former conscript from the southern town of Comodoro Rivadavia, found a job with the local council when he returned home and had five children. But at the age of thirty-seven, he hanged himself in a soccer stadium and left a note stating that he could not cope with his memories of the conflict. Jorge Martire, from La Plata, returned from the Falklands and barely spoke about what he had witnessed there. His wife said that he just wanted to forget about the war – like so many of us. The couple had three children and Jorge went to college to study architecture. Then, on his way to his final exam in October 1992, he suddenly disappeared. He was eventually found wandering around the city's main square. He had lost his memory and was subsequently treated for what the Argentinian veterans call the 'Malvinas syndrome'. During his stay in hospital, on one occasion doctors found Jorge hiding under his bed, sheltering from 'an English bombing'. When he was released in early 1993, he bought a gun, went to a bar and blew his head off in front of the horrified customers.

It had taken the fourteen thousand Argentinian veterans many years to organise themselves politically, but now several pressure groups were campaigning on their behalf. Peniel Villarreal, a spokesperson for the Federation of War Veterans of Argentina, explained, 'When we returned, we were ignored. We were nobodies. Nobody wanted to talk to us, give us healthcare or jobs.' Around half of the Argentinian veterans are still unemployed. 'We came back from a campaign where our friends were killed to a country that viewed us as letting them down. That's why more than four hundred of our colleagues have taken their own lives.'

Peniel vividly remembered the terrifying end of his Falklands War:

I was injured when a mortar landed on my foot in the battle for Goose Green. It blew away the legs of my companion and I thought I was dead. I was taken to a hospital ship, the *Uganda*, where I begged them not to kill me. The doctor told me: 'I am here to cure you, not to kill you.' He did. He saved the foot and I owe him my life. We were treated well by the British.

After much campaigning, the veterans have finally won recognition for their plight, and they now receive pensions and healthcare. But PTSD is still a major problem in Argentina, as Dr Viviana Torresi, of the Post-Traumatic Stress Disorder Centre, explained:

This condition, if not treated in time, tends to get worse. Patients have developed other pathologies related to post-traumatic stress disorder as a means to alleviate symptoms. One of the most common is insomnia, so they resort to alcohol as a sedative. Alcoholism, and many other addictions, is an answer to the lack of therapeutic treatment and professional care. The most painful experience these people had to go through was social abandon, and that was the only way many of them could cope with it.

At the barbecue in Plomer, Reinaldo told me a story that affected me deeply. While ferrying supplies to his comrades, he had heard a rumour that an entire company of forty-two men had been killed by Gurkhas. Allegedly, the dreaded hill-men had crept up on the Argies while they were sleeping and had slaughtered them with their *kukris*. According to the story, the Argies were all sleeping because their officer had kept them awake for days on end without a break. This story was notable for two reasons: its demonisation of the Gurkhas and its suggestion that Argentinian soldiers were badly mistreated by their own officers.

The latter was a recurring theme, and I became increasingly horrified as I heard more of the accusations that the veterans' organisations were levelling against the army. Most of these have been made by conscripts who were at the mercy of an officer corps that became desensitised to brutality during the six-year Dirty War. Some of the Argentinian NCOs and officers who served in the Falklands certainly had blood on their hands – the blood of their own people. The veterans have launched court proceedings against some of these men, with the most serious relating to killing and torturing their own men. One corporal is accused of murdering a soldier with a machine gun after an argument, several soldiers are said to have starved to death, and many others were staked out for hours in wet and freezing conditions. Staking out seems to have been a routine punishment in the Falklands, with the victims now known as the '*estaqueros*' – the staked-out ones.

Ernesto Alonso, secretary for institutional relations at the Centre for Ex-Combatants of the Malvinas Islands in La Plata, has been at the forefront of the campaign to bring seventy former officers to justice. He explained that while the veterans have now secured some concessions from the government, they are largely a case of too little, too late:

> It's like a medical emergency. If the doctor gets there in the first ten minutes, he saves your life. After that, the complications begin. If they had tried to support us in the first ten years, things would have been different. The war was improvised. The junta wanted the invasion to distract people from resistance to the regime. We were cannon fodder in a war we could not win. We lived in terrible conditions. We did not have proper equipment or sufficient food supplies to survive the cold temperatures. We were in a situation of extreme hunger, so we robbed food or killed sheep. Our own officers were our greatest enemies. They supplied themselves with whisky from the pubs, but they weren't prepared for war. They disappeared when things got serious.

Pointing out that many of the officers had previously acted as torturers for the military dictatorship, Ernesto added:

> They used us recruits for their sadistic fantasies. Argentina has come to terms with the dictatorship's human rights violations, but the crimes committed during the Malvinas

War are still taboo. We were relegated by society, the military didn't take care of us, and at the start of the new democracy we were considered part of the military dictatorship. We didn't have anything to do with that. We just went to fight for the sovereignty of the Malvinas because we were performing compulsory military service. We were completely abandoned by the government. The country owes us.

Ernesto's charges were powerfully echoed by a former conscript, Michael Savage, who was forced to leave college and undertake his compulsory military service. One morning, his platoon was patrolling near the front line when they came across a terrible sight:

It was the coldest day of the war and, in the white snow, we saw a soldier staked to the ground. He was dying. I saw many conscripts treated the same way by their NCOs. We lived in flimsy tents in sub-zero temperatures and our officers refused to issue proper rations. We were starving and would steal food if we got the chance. If you were caught, they would peg you to the ground and leave you crucified for hours, even in temperatures of minus twenty, with rain and even shelling.

One evening, I was caught by a corporal stealing a tin of

meat. He made me kneel down and pointed his gun at my head. I was crying and begging him not to shoot. I cannot forgive our officers. They were our worst enemies, torturing us physically and psychologically.

When we came home, nobody wanted to know. Society looked at us as part of the dictatorship, and the dictatorship looked at us as witnesses of a crime who had to be silenced.

Human rights activist Dr Pablo Vassel has also been involved in the campaign to bring Argentinian officers and NCOs to justice. He said:

We have testimonies from twenty-three people about a soldier who was shot to death by a corporal, four other former combatants who starved to death, and at least fifteen cases of conscripts who were staked out on the ground. The families were told the soldiers had been killed in combat. Soldiers were also the victims of unfair distribution of food and negligence from those in charge. Not one officer died of hunger, yet next to them some soldiers died of starvation.

The floodgates for all of these accusations opened with the publication of Edgardo Esteban's book and the subsequent film. Esteban has been more successful in life than most former conscripts. He lives in a secure suburb of Buenos Aires and is a well-known television correspondent. His study is covered with photographs relating to the success of his film, including one of himself with Robert de Niro. He has an easy charm and delights in showing off his well-stocked wine cellar. However, for all of his personal achievements, Edgardo remains indignant about the treatment of his fellow veterans, and he has bravely continued to accuse the army of bullying, starving and even sexually abusing the young conscripts. He said:

The main problem stems from the fact the Argentinian Army never acknowledged its errors and blamed the conscripts for the defeat. Argentinian society, which originally supported the invasion, abandoned us and linked us to the military dictatorship. When the conflict ended, there was no help. We were eighteen years old and thinking of returning home, settling, having a family, but instead we had to face death, anguish, depression, pain. When we were in the barracks, they made us sign an agreement to keep quiet. So, with society silencing us, and the silence we had in our hearts, it was very distressing.

Now is the time for justice. Without justice, it is impossible to reclaim the story of the Malvinas and the heroes who were there and fought with dignity.

After my visit to Argentina, Edgardo sent me a copy of his book, which I had translated into English. When I read it, I fully appreciated – probably for the first time – the absolute terror we had inflicted on the young Argentinian conscripts. It is a sad and moving story, powerfully told. In the book, Edgardo describes the hell of coming under bombardment:

That was when I wished I could become a cockroach, so as to slip between the rocks and leave this shitty place to look for a hole where no one would find me; perhaps I could open a crack in the wall and keep myself safe there until it was all over. My trousers were soaked in urine, and I realised that I had wet myself. My fear of loneliness had quickly become a fear of dying. I began to pray, remembering all the saints and my father. I asked him to help me, asked him to be with me so that I wouldn't die here alone. Who would come to find me? My greatest fear was to be injured and not be able to call for help. It was horrible to think that my survival depended solely on luck. I was exposed to death by pure chance.

You could tell which were the missiles by the whistling sound they made. But there were so many of them that you didn't know how to protect yourself. They shot ten of them at a time, and not only from the boats; by this point, we were visible targets for the infantry, so they were bombing us from all angles and we were entirely unprotected.

I was crossing a bare field, and I knew that coming out of all this alive was a matter of luck. The second I heard the whine of a missile, I threw myself to the ground, as if I was trying to bury myself among the wetland plants. Seconds later, a foxhole about three hundred metres from me exploded. With the blast, I saw the silhouettes of two soldiers go flying through the air. I felt that I could pick out those final cries from the rest of the noise, followed by the split-second silence of death, which was soon interrupted by other explosions. That silence after the cries seemed an eternity at the time, but it can't have lasted for more than five seconds. The visual impact of that scene – a scene where possible comrades of mine were blasted out their foxholes – felt like having my entrails ripped out. After witnessing something like that, it feels like you'll be empty for ever.

We were lying flat on the ground with our noses full of the smell of wet peat, chewing fervently on our crucifixes. We asked God to keep helping us so that those metal monsters wouldn't touch our poor bodies. I prayed to my father again, asking him to prevent my death from heaven, and prayed to all the virgins and saints in this blessed, cruel world that they would come down and save me. Only the odd morbid joke interrupted the brief silences between one explosion and another.

Edgardo recorded how their officers had initially tried to bolster morale by predicting doom for the British:

We believed Colonel Espíndola, who would tell anyone who would listen his theory that ours was the optimal situation. 'Imagine,' he said, 'we've been here waiting and readying ourselves for over a month. The British, on the other hand, have been on boats. Imagine how worn out they'll be, coming so far on a ship with the sole aim of making trouble on these islands! When those guys get here they'll be clueless and apathetic. Besides, we know every pebble of the terrain. They have no idea what they've got themselves into. They're not even used to the cold. No, lads! Those guys were dead meat from the beginning.'

How wrong could he be? The officers' next tactic was to try to frighten the conscripts into fighting by lying that the Gurkhas were raping, castrating and shooting prisoners, but that was pretty counter-productive, too:

They told us that the Gurkhas were wreaking havoc, that they had slit the throats of a whole company of Regiment

7, and that they killed at close range. The soldiers were saying that the English were homing in on us like wild animals, and that they were drugged up. The tales that they told us only made us more terrified and multiplied our hatred for those sons of bitches. They were advancing and killing, and they weren't going to stop until we were wiped out.

Like so many of us, Edgardo left the Falklands with a troubled mind – a lasting souvenir of the war in which so many of his comrades and friends had died. He describes one of his nightmares in the book:

I saw the eyes of my fellow soldier, Vallejos, who was dying in front of me as if he wanted to say something to me. Vallejos's body was sprawled out on top of a mound of damp earth, dying without even being able to cry out because he was covered in blood all over, and the hole that the shrapnel had made in his stomach was gushing blood out everywhere. When he tried to speak, he choked on his own blood, which poured from his open mouth like a drowned scream, blood mixed with the mud that the explosions were blasting all over the place. And there was Vallejos, saying goodbye, with those terrified, surprised eyes gazing at me. My friend, poor Vallejos, was lying in his foxhole with the smell of hot blood and shit and rotten food – that unforgettable smell which clung to the insides of my nostrils for an eternity. The guilt I felt for Vallejos's death was like a splinter embedded in my flesh.

Over the past thirty years, thousands of men – from both sides – have suffered similar nightmares about that short, sharp, brutish war in the South Atlantic.

Estimates of the total number of veteran suicides vary. But it is likely that around five hundred Argentinians and three hundred British ex-servicemen have taken their own lives since 1982. And that does not include those who have died of drink-, drugs- or poverty-related problems. It is dreadful to think that after all these years – three decades – men from both sides are still suffering and dying as a direct result of the conflict.

My trip to Argentina was an eye-opener in many ways. It allowed me to put my own reaction to the war into perspective and helped me understand just how typical my struggle with PTSD had been. I also now appreciated how the Argentinian people felt about the islands that lay just five hundred kilometres off their shore and fifteen thousand from ours.

But I still could not decide if the war had been worth all

the suffering. Did we pay too high a price to keep possession of this little group of islands? There seemed only one way to find an answer. I realised I had to revisit the battlefields of the Falklands.

CHAPTER 8

BACK TO THE BATTLEFIELD

When I decided to go back to the Falklands, the *Secret Millionaire* team asked if they could come down and film my return for a second programme. The resulting documentary – *How Secret Millionaire Changed My Life* – was one of only two sequels to be made for the series. It was certainly a lot less stressful than the original programme. The former battle-grounds of the Falklands were a lot more welcoming than the current battleground in Anfield. After the first episode, my old mate Wayne Rees had got in touch with me. It had been great to meet up, so I decided to invite him and another veteran, Jim Foster – an ex-medic – to come with me. The idea was to visit the old battlefields and tab once again to Goose Green.

As the time drew near, I became increasingly excited at the prospect. It felt unreal to be going back, but then so had been my trip to Argentina to meet people we had once tried to kill. When we went to the RAF base at Brize Norton, I suddenly realised that it was the first time I had been back there since I'd left the army. It brought back great memories of my early TA days and of all those jumps. It is now the main departure point by air for our troops, and as I sat in the bar, having a beer with Jim and Wayne, we saw all these squaddies getting ready to fly out to Afghanistan. My God, I thought, They are just kids. Just like we were. It was scary. Seeing those teenagers brought back all the old memories. Here we were, nearly thirty years on, still sending young boys off to remote and rugged places to be killed and maimed. How many would come back in one piece? And what sort of mental damage would they sustain? Were they fully aware of the dangers of the unseen wounds in the mind that might not manifest themselves for more than a decade but would blight their lives and the lives of those around them?

'Was it all worth it?' I wondered. I had serious doubts. I didn't think we had achieved much in Iraq. And as for Afghanistan, I was sceptical that we would succeed where the Red Army, Alexander the Great and the British Empire had all failed. But of course I admired the courage and professionalism of the young soldiers who were going out to lay their lives on the line. Seeing those lads embark also made me wonder about the value of our war in the Falklands. It had happened long before most of these young soldiers had been born. Had it been worth all of the pain and anguish, the death and disability . . . on both sides? I still had to make my mind up about that. But over the past year I had certainly come to question the value of a war in which one thousand men died for a group of desolate, windswept islands in the middle of nowhere.

From Brize Norton, we flew to Ascension Island on a primitive Air Seychelles plane. We stopped at the American base on Ascension, disembarked, and were herded into what they call the 'pig pen' while the aircraft refuelled. We were not allowed to leave the caged area so just hung around before taking off for the Falklands. Descending into the new airport at RAF Mount Pleasant was something else. It is a massive airfield and a vital part of the British Forces South Atlantic Islands (BFSAI) set-up. The station – which lies about thirty miles south-west of Stanley, on East Falkland – is home to between one and two thousand British military personnel at any one time. The barracks, messes, and recreational and welfare areas of the base are linked by what is reputed to be the world's longest corridor – it's about half a mile long. The locals know the base as the 'Death Star' because it is so sprawling and so easy to get lost inside. We were told that it was initially meant to be only a temporary base, but it had morphed into a permanent structure.

After landing, we were picked up by guys in Land-Rovers and headed due west, to Darwin. The settlement lies on Choiseul Sound, on the east side of the island's central isthmus, two and a half miles north of Goose Green. It took a good couple of hours to get there, but the roads, while not metalled, were quite reasonable. They had not even existed the last time I had been there. As we drove, I took in the landscape and was struck by the sheer vastness of the place. People, including me, forget the islands are the size of Wales. We had generally gone everywhere by night and had focused only on the 150 metres either side of us.

As we pulled into Darwin, it looked just the same. It was amazing that nothing much had changed. It seemed as if we were in a time warp – there were no modern structures at all. Even in Goose Green, the sheds where we kept the POWs still had that abbreviation painted on the roof. One of the guys who drove us had been the chief constable on the islands. He was an English guy who had since retired and now ran a B&B in Darwin. We joked with him that being chief constable here must have been the easiest job ever. What did he have to deal with, apart from the odd stolen sheep? 'Who the bloody hell comes here?' we asked. He told us we'd be surprised – the place was a real hot-spot for bird watchers. True enough, right on cue, a crowd of twitchers appeared with huge telephoto lenses on their cameras. Each of them was probably worth £20,000. They were catching a flight to a far-flung island in the hope of getting a peek at some rare bird.

We stayed at the ex-chief's B&B and the next day went to visit San Carlos Bay. The Blue Beach military cemetery, overlooking the bay, was immaculately kept and a far cry from the muddy mass grave where we had laid the boys to rest immediately after the Battle of Goose Green. Most of the families had asked for the bodies of their loved ones to be repatriated, but fourteen graves remained. Among them were four paras, including Colonel H Jones, who had a VC carved on his stone. I had known all four of them. As we paid our respects at the cemetery, I could still hear Padre Cooper's northern tones battling against the Antarctic winds as we buried the men all those years ago.

Next we went up the Sussex Mountains and identified the outlines of some of those miserable shell-scrapes where we had frozen our nuts off. After some searching, we located the exact spot where we had dug in on the side of the mountain and fired our arc of fire at those Argie jets that had come in to paste the ships below. The memories were so vivid. It seemed like yesterday. We walked over the mountain to Camilla Creek and met a couple who were cooking eggshells in an oven to be ground down and mixed with their chicken feed. It was all so peaceful now. From the battle start line at the creek, we walked to Goose Green. We did the same walk that we had tabbed – twice – all those years ago. Now, though, there were roads, which meant it was much easier going – none of the dreaded moongrass for us this time. During the walk, we tried to work out our exact route. We had books to remind us and we eventually pieced it together. We reminisced as we went and visited the precise spot – a small gully – where Steve Dixon had died. I had a few moments of silent reflection there. It was very emotional. It brought it all back and I relived that awful moment when I saw the life drain out of a young man who had his whole future in front of him. It had been so horrific, and I had never been able to get it completely out of my mind since.

Everywhere we looked, there seemed to be signs warning of minefields. Back in 1982, we had known nothing about mines. We must have walked right between them! It was probably best we had not known about them at the time. We went to where the schoolhouse had been and to the spot near the airfield where we had been pinned down. We relaxed as we went and some of the old para banter returned.

When we walked into Goose Green, we found that it had not changed in three decades, either. Near by, we found a single grave surrounded by a freshly painted wooden fence and guarded by two small, wind-battered trees. It looked so lonely and poignant. It was the final resting place of thirty-two-year-old Lieutenant Nick Taylor, who died on 4 May 1982 when his Sea Harrier was shot down by the Argies. The gravestone read: 'In proud memory of a dearly loved husband, son and brother, shot down while flying for the country he loved.' Farm workers from the settlement still tend the grave and keep it beautifully maintained.

We were given a great reception at the community hall where we had discovered all of the incarcerated locals. It was incredible. All of the villagers were there and they were so genuinely grateful for what we had done. It was really interesting to talk with them. Some of them had been children at the time and were obviously now in their thirties and forties. The older ones talked about hiding under the floorboards in their homes during the bombardments. One guy, an ex-schoolteacher, mentioned the liberation. I asked how he'd felt when it was over and he replied, 'You'll never know what it feels like. You've never been occupied, let alone liberated. The last occupation of Britain was in 1066 after the Battle of Hastings. It's so hard to put into words – the elation and the feelings we had.' I remembered the Dutch crowds who had mobbed our vehicles as we drove through Holland to exercise in Germany before I'd even heard of the Falklands. For them, the elation of liberation had been so strong that they were still expressing it decades later. Now, the same was true here.

From Goose Green, we went to Fitzroy. As we walked along the beach where we had helped to treat the burned and shocked Welsh Guards, the mood became more sombre. We looked at the memorials, and Jim Foster had his own moment there to remember a friend who was killed in that bleak place. We went to the sheep sheds and found that they were just the same. Internally, they were identical, but I was surprised to find that they were so far from the beach. The dash to help the guys from the stricken *Sir Galahad* had been much further than I remembered. We must have been really pumped with adrenalin when we raced down to get the boys ashore.

In 1982, landing in the Falklands was like stepping back in time. Stanley, the capital, had a 1950s feel to it. Of course, the war took its toll on the town, but the place had clearly been in decline long before then. The population was ageing and there were very few young people around. It seemed to be down on its luck. The islanders relied on low-value sales of wool and were insecure because of years of Argie sabre-rattling and British indecision and dithering. A lot of the big sheep stations were owned by UK-based landowners and the place had a neglected feel to it. Now, though, Port Stanley was positively booming. Britain had declared a two-hundred-mile fishing zone around the islands and the Falklanders were raking in millions each year from the sale of licences. Tourism was on the increase, too, with cruise ships putting in regularly. The service personnel stationed on the islands were also spending in the community. The upshot was that the Falklands had a balance of trade surplus that Britain could only dream of – and this was *before* the upsurge in oil exploration that promises to deliver an even bigger bonanza to the islanders.

It was great to see the progress the islands had made. Maybe our sacrifices had been worthwhile after all. The Falklands had become economically self-sufficient and had put their new-found wealth to good use. Port Stanley had almost doubled in size and boasted its first secondary school, a swimming pool, new medical facilities and a modern hotel. The population of the islands had almost doubled, too. It still felt very British, with Union Flags flying everywhere, pubs where you could get a good pint, and cafés selling fish and chips. New streets had been named after Margaret Thatcher and our commander, Sir Jeremy Moore, while the older ones were named after places like Glasgow and Kent. Young islanders were sent to Britain to be educated, with their college and university fees paid by the Falkland Islands government. And they usually returned to the islands to set themselves up as doctors, teachers and pilots – jobs that had once gone to incomers. There was a confidence about the place, and the islanders were certainly making the most of their opportunities.

It was great to visit Liberty Lodge, a self-catering lodge built by the Falklands Veterans Foundation to accommodate visiting veterans. It is a fantastic resource and I feel that we veterans are very lucky to have it. After all, the lads who fought in Afghanistan, Iraq, the Balkans and Sierra Leone will never have the opportunity to stay somewhere similar. It was yet another indicator of how much the islanders appreciated our sacrifice.

The Argentinian government has been ratcheting up the tension that surrounds the islands' future in recent years, with one of its most frequent assertions being that many of the islanders have been implanted by the British government. Nothing could be further from the truth. I met numerous islanders whose families had lived there for generations. Among them was sixty-eight-year-old Neil Watson, whose family had lived on the Falklands since arriving from Scotland with the first British colonial expedition in 1840. Galtieri's troops arrived two years to the day after Neil had bought his very own stake in the islands. On 2 April 1980, the Falkland Islands government had organised a special ceremony at Government House, with Rex Hunt presiding. Neil was one of the first beneficiaries of a progressive scheme that allowed islanders to buy small farms in a bid to weaken the grip of the large absentee landowners. He is now the proud owner of Long Island Farm, a 22,000-acre sheep station twenty miles from Stanley that includes part of Mount Longdon.

Short but still very fit, Neil is a no-nonsense, down-to-earth farmer with a great sense of humour. But it was stretched to breaking point when Argentina invaded. He recalled:

Throughout the occupation, I was consumed by a deep feeling of anger. I was naturally worried for the children, but apart from that my main emotion was anger. I was angry all the time. The adrenalin always seemed to be flowing and some nights I could not sleep because I was so angry.

Personally, I had been expecting the invasion, so it was not a shock to me, but seeing all these Argies going about was a bit strange. There had been loads of indications that an invasion was imminent. In fact, I told my wool agent in the UK not to send me a cheque but to bank it in the UK as we feared invasion. That was three months before the Argies landed!

To begin with, they were OK. We have a stretch of beach here and they thought the British might use it as a landing point, so heavy machine-gun and mortar positions were set up on the ridge above the farm. We had to negotiate Argentinian checkpoints on the track into Stanley but then, as the war progressed, we were locked down on the farm. It didn't bother us too much because we are self-sufficient, with peat fires for heating and plenty of beef and lamb around. We also have very productive vegetable gardens. But then they started killing cattle and sheep to eat and tearing down fences for firewood. They were a bloody nuisance.

Neil had trained with the Falkland Islands Defence Force, and the last six British marines to be captured after the invasion had surrendered at his farm. The Argies had their suspicions about Neil and special units began to arrive by helicopter to raid the farm and search the outbuildings. They were not bad judges, because Neil was one of the heroes of the Falklands resistance. The Argies never found the weapons that the marines had buried on his farm.

Neil's involvement in the liberation of the islands began with a knock at the door one dark evening:

I thought, Bloody Argies on the scrounge again! and answered the door. I opened it to find a blacked-up Englishman standing on the doorstep. 'Who the fuck are you?' I asked. It was obvious he was not the man from Milk Tray. It turned out they were a bunch of very nice lads from the Special Boat Service. It was great to see them. I was so elated when the British landed at San Carlos, totally elated. The SBS boys slept outside that night and didn't come into the farmhouse except for the odd cup of tea. There had been a lot of enemy activity up on the ridge that day, with Huey helicopters coming and going. We didn't know how many Argies were up there. In the morning, we looked up but couldn't see anything. So I decided to ride up on my horse with the sheepdogs to check it out. The place was deserted – they had all buggered off, presumably to reinforce Goose Green.

That night, I drove the lads five miles across country in my Land-Rover with no headlights in the pitch dark in fairly boggy conditions. It was pretty exciting. The SBS guys made a rendezvous at a creek and departed in high-speed raiding boats into the darkness. Years later, one of them came back and presented me with an SBS plaque. It is one of my most precious possessions and hangs proudly on my wall.

Neil was also a member of a twenty-strong team of islanders who loaded up their tractors and trailers with ammunition and kit for 3 Para and drove up to the start line for the Battle of Mount Longdon. It was a dangerous operation and the civilians came under fire from tracers and shells.

It was great to hear of the assistance that they had given to the war effort. I could really identify with these people. They were a hardy, self-reliant bunch and had been prepared to do their bit. Neil had even used a bit of psychological warfare on his unwanted guests:

I felt a bit sorry for some of the conscripts. They were poorly trained, just doing their national service. A couple of them used to come down here to cadge water. There was plenty of water up there on the hill but they wanted to drink water that came out of a tap. One was a trainee priest and the other was a trainee dentist. I was fed up to the back teeth with the occupation, though, so one day I breezily told them, 'Oh, can you tell the major that the Gurkhas have landed. I am sure he would be interested to know.' They were shit scared of the Gurkhas. They looked aghast to hear this news and immediately dashed off to tell the major. I had a chuckle to myself as they tore up the hill.

I never had any doubts that the British would win. When I heard that the paras and the marines were on their way, backed up by the Scots and Welsh Guards and the Gurkhas, I thought, The Argies have had it now. Some of them felt like that, too. Shortly after they arrived, one of the Argentinian officers asked if he could come in and listen to the BBC World Service. When he heard the report on the task force leaving the Channel his jaw dropped and almost bounced off his shiny boots.

Neil was lucky not to be arrested or exiled to Fox Bay –
a remote spot on West Falkland where other members of the
Falkland Islands Defence Force were sent. The Falklanders
exiled there spent much of the war incommunicado, not
knowing whether their families were safe during the fierce
fighting, shelling and bombing. It was obviously a trying
time for them.

Gerald Cheek was a resident of Port Stanley who was
plucked from his family home and taken away by the occupiers. He explained:

I was forty-one when the invasion happened. I was in
the Falkland Islands Defence Force, which is very similar
to the TA. We were told by the Governor to surrender
to the Argentinians and that is what we did. Three weeks
into the conflict, I was taken away to West Falkland and
I spent the next seven weeks there. Ten weeks might
not seem like a long time, but it was a long, long ten
weeks for us. Although, when you think the British
had eight thousand miles to travel, I suppose it is pretty
short.

I lived with my wife, Marie, and my daughters Diane
and Barbara, who were fourteen and ten at the time.
Being taken away from them was really, really hard. It was
very distressing, to say the least. I didn't know where I was

going or what was going to happen to me. The military police just came to the house and told me to come with them. When I asked what would happen to my elderly parents, they said, 'Do you want to be taken alone?' I had to make a pretty quick decision. I didn't know where I was going and feared I might be taken to Argentina. Maybe we would be used as hostages? All kinds of thoughts raced through my mind. But they took us to the other island, West Falkland. It was OK. We lived on a farm and we were not harassed by the Argentinians. They didn't give us much bother – they just didn't want us to have any kind of communication. But we managed to keep a radio hidden away and we used to listen to broadcasts on the BBC. It was like being in Nazi-occupied Europe. We had to hide it every time the Argentinian major came across. It was on the BBC that we heard the Argentinians had been told to surrender from their HQ in Stanley. Two days later, a British naval helicopter came and brought us back to Stanley.

Stanley was in a bit of a state when we got back. I was shocked. There was lots of destruction and some buildings had been shelled. It was a real mess. It was fantastic to see the family, though. There was great jubilation when I came back to the house – the girls ran to me straight away. They were surprised to see me because we had had no communication since 21 April, and this was 16 June.

Like all of the islanders I met, Gerald was emphatic that the Falklands should remain British and should never be ceded to Argentina. He said:

The islands have changed over the past thirty years. They are quite mixed now. We have quite a lot of Chilean workers but mostly it is British people. There are some Argentinians. Some of them are married to local people. I have no antagonism towards them, just towards the Argentinian government. They keep putting pressure on the islanders. But we don't ever want to become Argentinian. For a while, Argentina was a military dictatorship and thirty thousand people were killed. They were throwing people out of aircraft across the South Atlantic. I want nothing to do with that. They aren't like that at the moment but they still don't treat people well. We're quite happy to remain British. We are British and always will be – no matter what rubbish we hear from the Argentinians. They have never owned the islands. The British discovered them. Every year, Argentina tells the UN that its people were thrown off the islands but that is just not true. There are so many lies.

I was intrigued by Neil Watson's tale of local farmers help-ing 3 Para and wanted to hear more about it. My enquiries took me to Brookfield Farm and a memorable meeting with the redoubtable Trudi McPhee – a fifth-generation islander whose ancestors had arrived in the South Atlantic from the Hebridean island of Harris. During the war, Trudi – who was twenty-four at the time – played an outstanding role in organ-ising her fellow islanders in support of the British, and specifically 3 Para. She recalled:

There had been rumblings for years and years and years, but we never expected to be invaded. Then the radio advised us that the Governor was to make a special announcement. When Rex Hunt announced that inva-sion was imminent, we were scared. We never slept that night and were very on edge. Every shooting star was an Argie plane. When they did arrive, it was very frighten-ing for the old people. This is one of the quietest places on earth and all of a sudden all hell broke out and we had thousands of Argie soldiers with their heavy armour and guns. They issued all kinds of edicts about what we could do and what we couldn't do. They cut off the telephones and banned the use of CB radios, which people relied on here. It was bloody awful. We were under military occu-pation. They had American mercenaries with them who enjoyed sticking guns in people's backs as they searched their houses.

I was so angry about them invading but could not do much about it. Every time an Argie helicopter flew overhead, I would rush out and wave my frying pan at them, shouting, 'Argie bastards!' It was all I could do.

Before long, though, Trudi was taking a more active role in the resistance:

One day, Terry Peck turned up at the house and asked if we would put him up. He explained that he was on the run. He was the former chief constable on the islands and had been spying on the Argies for British intelligence. He was tipped off that he was going to be arrested and legged it. The Argies believed that he had been SAS trained, so they were desperate to catch him. I told him that I could not put him up as we had children present and the Argies had already warned us that our families would suffer if we were caught helping the British. But we fed him and dropped off food to him at prearranged points every day.

Peck worked closely with the British in the run-up to the Battle of Mount Longdon, while Trudi acted as his link with the rest of the community:

He told me to get as many people together with vehicles as I could and get up to the *estancia* [sheep station] near Longdon. We assembled a fleet of six tractors, fourteen tracked vehicles and nine Land-Rovers and spent the next two weeks driving paratroopers, bullets, ammunition, food, water and medical supplies across country. On 11 June, the second-in-command of 3 Para told us things were getting sticky and we all had to write a last letter in case we didn't make it. It made us think a bit but it didn't stop us.

That night, Trudi led a convoy of Land-Rovers to transport vital medical supplies and paramedics to forward positions, where they were needed to treat the large numbers of serious casualties arising from the fighting and shelling on the mountain. The convoy came under enemy fire but pressed on. Trudi received an official military commendation for her role from task force chief Admiral Sir John Fieldhouse. She keeps it proudly to hand. It reads:

On 11 June she drove a Land-Rover in support of the 3rd Battalion the Parachute Regiment operation to secure Mount Longdon. Travelling across the most appalling terrain, without lights, she drove one of only three Land-Rovers which successfully arrived at the mortar line [.] At times under enemy artillery, she remained resolved to continue, showing tremendous steadfastness in dangerous and unfamiliar circumstances.

Most of the islanders I met had developed some sympathy for the suffering of the Argie conscripts, but Trudi was not one of them. She still felt incredibly angry about the invasion and had no interest in any kind of reconciliation. Instead, she kept a warm welcome and an open house for returning British veterans. She said, 'Most of the islanders really appreciate how those young guys gave their lives for our freedom. We will never forget what those guys did for us. We can never thank them enough.' It was good to know that our efforts were still appreciated after all these years.

It would have been great to meet Terry Peck. He was a real hero, and was awarded an MBE for his courage during the conflict. But I was saddened to hear that he had suffered from PTSD before his death in 2006.

For many Falklanders, the invasion was still remembered as much more than an inconvenient episode during which the Argies changed street names, ordered Spanish to be spoken in the schools, and insisted that everybody drive on the right-hand side of the road. As the British task force steamed steadily closer, the noose tightened around the necks of the local population. A curfew was introduced and rigorously enforced. It was dangerous to go out after dark as nervous Argie soldiers thought they saw a British commando or Gurkha lurking behind every bush. House-to-house searches became more common, frightening young and old alike. People were arrested, held in cells and interrogated. Sometimes their families did not know what had happened to them, so they inevitably feared that their loved ones had joined the ranks of the 'disappeared ones'.

Isabel Castle was not alone in finding the invasion a miserable and frightening experience:

I was thirty-four during the occupation. There was just my husband, David, and me. We didn't have any children. We had moved down here from Oxford five years before the invasion, looking for peace and quiet. When the war broke out, we didn't know what to expect. It was a complete shock. A friend phoned me around midnight on the night things all began and started speaking in code words. I didn't understand and eventually she told me to look over at the harbour, which was full of Argie troops. I didn't think anything of it but all through the night I heard gunfire. It was terrifying. The next day, we were visited by a major from the Argentinian Army. They came into the house. It was awful. I didn't want them in my home.

My husband was the director of the West Store, the town supermarket, and that is where we ended up sleeping. At one point, near the end of the conflict, there were seventy of us living there. We always had to be back by 4 p.m., so we had to go home for a wash and get back before the curfew. My husband was pushed up against the wall nearly every night by the Argentinians. The worst thing that ever happened to me occurred one morning at around 6 a.m. We were all brought out of the supermarket and lined up against a wall by the Argentinians. They had guns and I thought we were going to be shot. But other people went through an awful lot more than I did.

We always say that we wouldn't want to go through it again, but that we are glad we didn't leave. This is our home, and we stand by that. This is Britain, after all. It has never been Argentina. A few people who served here with the British forces during the conflict have since come and settled. We don't associate with the Argentinians. I shouldn't say this, but we get a lot of Argentinian tourism here and a lot of them come ashore and they're not the nicest. They have this attitude that the Falkland Islands – or Islas Malvinas, as they call them – are theirs. But if you look back, they have never been Argentinian. They've been owned by Spain and France, but never Argentina.

In the days after the liberation – when we were dealing with prisoners, tidying the place up and packing our kit to return home – we did not have much of a chance to speak to the islanders. Meanwhile, the locals were trying to rebuild their lives and getting on with things. So it was fantastic to hear all of their stories now. They were stories of resistance, determination and defiance, but they were often told with humour. For the first time, I began to feel that we – troops and islanders – had all been in it together.

Hulda Stewart comes from a long-established Falklands family. She was a schoolteacher when the islands were invaded:

It was extremely scary when the Governor announced on local radio in the early evening that a task force from Argentina was heading our way and that the Falkland Islands would be invaded by morning. We are relatively small islands in the middle of a giant ocean. We are not close to anybody. It was a dreadful feeling, not knowing what was going to happen. We really thought most of us would be killed. After all, this was an army that had been killing its own people. We didn't know the Argies would try to win our hearts and minds. We went to a neighbour's house and drank coffee while we endlessly talked over the possibilities. The Argies obviously landed people before morning because that night somebody went into our greenhouse and stole some of our tomatoes. That sort of thing never happened in Stanley.

My sister Rita had married one of the marines who were stationed in the Falklands. She was in Carnoustie in Scotland with a young son while we were all over here, and her husband was fighting here. So she stood to lose her whole family. She was in a dreadful state. During the fighting, which we could hear all around us, we were worried for her husband. We knew he was here, but we didn't know if he had been injured, or killed, or anything.

Nevertheless, in a typically British response to the invasion, Hulda kept a stiff upper lip and was determined to keep doing her job. She recalled:

The Argentinians took over parts of the school and we didn't know how safe it was to use it. So I got my Land-Rover and collected as many schoolchildren as I could every morning and brought them to my house on the fringes of Port Stanley, where we could have some lessons. It gave the parents a little bit of breathing space. It was very good for the children, too. They say that they don't like school, but when they can't go, they find that they actually do like it. Iain, my late husband, used to go in his car and get some children, too. We also collected elderly people and brought them up for afternoon tea. They were very nervous and very isolated, so this gave them the opportunity to relax for a few hours and talk to other people. Falklanders never locked their doors back then – some still don't – and my aunt had just finished baking lots of little cakes when an Argentinian conscript dashed in, grabbed the cakes and left. The older people were very, very fearful.

When the Argentinians heard that we were having all these children and older people round, they spoke to my husband and asked if we were running a spy ring. We were astounded. It was ridiculous that they thought all these old people walking about with sticks were spies, really quite ridiculous. Old-age spies! But that was the Argentinian mentality.

We were sometimes scared, but we couldn't just sit back and do nothing. My husband was an engineer at the major telecommunications provider in the Falklands, which had been taken over. What terrified me was that he had brought home diagrams showing how some things worked and had hidden them in the foundations of our house. He had done this because he wanted to thwart the Argentinians in any way he could. He was told by the chief intelligence officer, 'We know you are up to something, and we will find out.' It was really scary.

People were trying to be as difficult as possible with the Argies without antagonising them too much. They were becoming really quite nasty before the liberation. Early on, they had tried to befriend us, but towards the end they became noticeably different. It was very frightening.

Hulda and her husband welcomed some guys from 3 Para into their home not long after the bloody Battle of Mount Longdon:

When the ceasefire came, nobody quite knew what was going on. We were staying with my brother in the town, having left our house on the outskirts when the fighting got nearer. Iain and I went out somewhere and when we got back my mother had obviously found out that there was a ceasefire and it was hopefully all over. It was quite amusing. We're not Roman Catholic, but a priest had called in and there was my mother and him in his robes, both dancing around the kitchen. They were so elated. It was quite strange that evening. Iain and I just wanted to get back home to see what was happening. We heard rumours that there were paras around the area and, sure enough, we found about thirty or forty in our house. That was really something. I'll never forget that – a lot of them still had blood on their faces.

Right away, the man in charge asked if this was our house and did we want them to move out. We said of course not, after all they had done. Most of our windows had been broken by shrapnel and bullets. I started to make tea for them. They were all young lads and you could see a lot of them were in a state of shock. I told one of them that I was having trouble with the Primus stove and asked if he could help me to get it working. He said he was hopeless with Primuses but that he would go and get his mate. After a second or two, he walked back in and there was an anguished look of naked vulnerability on his face. He said bleakly, 'I can't ask him. He died at Longdon.' It must have receded to the back of his mind for a second. It is a memory that haunts me still.

Another of the young paras in the house that night was called Graham Tolson. He told me that the night before the attack on Mount Longdon, his mate had had a premonition that he would die, so he had given Graham letters for his wife and family. Sure enough, the young guy was killed. Graham was devastated; it was so sad.

I tried to cook a big, hot meal at lunchtime the next day. We had vegetables in the garden and meat in the freezer. The guys had been living off rations, so I also got tins of biscuits and sweets that we had hidden from the Argentinians and made all these cakes. Everything in the house went quiet as they wolfed them down. But they didn't just eat all the cakes themselves: they kept some for their mates down the road. It was amazing.

Some of the paras have come back since and have said that they can't tell us what it meant to them – after living out in the cold and eating rations – to come into a house. But we could never do enough to repay them for what they did.

We have always been, and always will be, British. That was the one thing my dad said to me when we were growing up. He told us, 'The thing you should be most proud of in life is that we are British.' We feel very strongly about that. There are one or two hot-heads on the islands who stupidly talk about independence. That's obviously not possible. About 99.9 per cent of people see themselves as British and want to remain British. People here always talk about saving money to go 'home' – and by that they mean Britain, even though they were born in the Falkland Islands. They talk about when they were 'at home' on holiday. In some ways, we're more British than the British.

Hulda's brother, Patrick Watts, was a journalist with the Falklands' radio station during the invasion. Famously, he was broadcasting when the first Argies charged into his studio. In a moment that has entered the islands' folklore, he told the intruders to 'stop that racket and put those guns down'. He also told them to stop smoking. Amazingly, they did as instructed. Like many other Falklanders, Patrick displayed a strong streak of independence. Before talking about his experiences during the war, he wanted to stress that the Falklands were paying their own way. Moreover, he said that if oil was discovered and the islands were further enriched, they would be delighted to pay for their defence – which he was at pains to point out accounted for only half a per cent of total UK defence spending.

During the occupation, Patrick battled with his new Argentinian bosses to secure eight hours a day of English-language broadcasting. He also enjoyed winding up the Argies:

Quite often, officers would drop in to have a coffee and get out of the cold. A lot of them spoke English and most of them wanted nothing to do with fighting. They were not keen at all. They never thought the task force would cross the equator and believed that they had world opinion on their side. They thought it would end with negotiations. When the officers were leaving the station, our parting shot was always: 'Oh well, that's the task force another day nearer.' You could tell it depressed them. Everything changed when the *Belgrano* and the *Sheffield* were sunk. We thought, People are dying here. They are not fooling about.

As the fighting drew nearer to Port Stanley, the islanders formed a rudimentary civil defence force to try to protect themselves as best they could. Some houses, those built from stone rather than the more common timber, were designated 'safe houses'. People from outlying farms threatened by the fighting, or those who lived in timber houses in the town, bunked down in these places. Tragically, in one case, the system backfired.

John Fowler was the director of education on the islands, and his stone house was selected as one of the refuges. But in the very last days of fighting his home was caught in the blast of a 4.5-inch naval shell. Three women sheltering there were killed. Yet even John was convinced that Britain had been right to send the task force to the islands:

The invasion was a shocking thing for us. Stanley was such a quiet place that I used to compare it to a Scottish Sunday afternoon. The next thing we knew, we had six thousand troops digging in, storing ammunition in the school playground and driving round with heavy guns. Helicopters and jets were flying in and out, and the Argies sent a complete bastard – Major Patricio Dowling – to head up the police. He was of Irish descent and had a hatred of the British. We used to listen to the BBC World Service and when I heard that the task force was coming down I was totally delighted. The Argentinian officers would drop in to hear the news and you could tell that they were full of fear and apprehension.

As the fighting erupted around Stanley, we could see the tracers cutting across the night sky, and every evening at eight the navy would bombard the Argie positions. It felt surreal and I also started to feel a bit guilty that men were dying for us, for our freedom. But it was about British territorial integrity and the British government was sending a signal to the world, including the Russians, that it would not surrender that integrity.

Like most of Stanley's townspeople, John had vivid memories of the arrival of the Brits:

I was out in the street on my own when three hundred British soldiers suddenly drove into town. There was nobody else about. I thought of those newsreels of the liberation of Paris, with thousands of people in the Champs-Élysées cheering their liberators. This was very different, but it was my moment of liberation and I cherished it.

Wherever Wayne, Jim and I went in the town, we received a fantastic reception, especially when people heard we were from 2 Para. Even after all these years, the Falkland Islanders clearly remembered that we were first into Port Stanley. They just loved us. We attended a function at the Falkland Islands Defence Force Hall in Stanley and we literally could not buy a drink all night. Even when we insisted, the barman would not let us pay. Eventually, I had to force him to take thirty pounds for the charity box.

Later, we met the commander of the BFSAI and the Governor. I had a good chat with the commander, who had been a young sub-lieutenant in the Royal Navy during the war. He told me that they have to deal with some sort of bother from the Argies every single day. They might probe defences with their navy or air force, or just say something to the world's media. It sounded a bit like the Russians flying into British airspace during the Cold War. The commander said that every time a cruise ship comes into the Falklands, he sticks the Typhoons in the air and buzzes it, just to remind any South Americans on board that the British are there.

I find it sad that Argentina – despite now being a democratic nation – still does not recognise the democratic rights of the islanders. Relations between Britain and Argentina remain strained, and the Argentinians have persuaded other South American countries to blockade Falklands shipping. As a result, the islands are forced to rely on one flight a week from Chile, the twice-weekly flights from Britain, and the shipping link to the UK.

A mate of mine from Kirriemuir, Drew Irvine, has been in the Falklands for over twenty years and loves it. Naturally, I made a point of meeting up with him. His job is to look after the local fishing fleet, which means he has had to deal with a lot of Argentinian intransigence over the past two decades. He told us one story about a guy who was out at sea and fell seriously ill. The closest port for the trawler was in Argentina, but the authorities refused it entry. The guy who fell ill was Spanish, but the Argentinians were determined to make him suffer because he was on a British-owned vessel that was associated with the Falkland Islands.

As the plane home prepared for take-off, I took stock of our visit. I had not spoken much about the Falklands over the past thirty years, partly because I had been a bit cynical about the war. Also, it had not been as much of a popular cause in Scotland as it had been in England. For me, the war had been about me and my mates doing a job. That was all. My personal experience of the war had confirmed my detestation of armed conflict; and as I had learned of the terrible price that veterans in both Britain and Argentina were still paying, those convictions had grown stronger. The Argentinian veterans were ordinary blokes, just like us, and it seemed incredible and absurd that we had killed and maimed each other for the sake of a few tiny islands.

But this trip back to the Falklands was a revelation to me – almost a religious experience. Having met the islanders, I no longer felt guilty or cynical about the war. On the contrary, I felt proud to have helped in the liberation of British territory. I now knew for sure that it was a worthwhile cause, after all. And visiting the memorials and places where my pals had died had brought me a sense of peace and calm. So, when the aircraft took off, I was at ease with myself for the first time in a long time. Looking down on the islands as they became small dots in the grey vastness of the South Atlantic, I vowed that I would return, hopefully for a visit that was as peaceful as the one I had just enjoyed.

Unfortunately, though, Britain and Argentina were still at loggerheads over the islands' future. That left me with a tough question: what if there was another war?

After a moment's reflection, I knew the answer: I would fix bayonets and get stuck in. I would do it all over again.

ACKNOWLEDGEMENTS

I would like to thank Graham Ogilvy, senior writer at Scottish News Agency, for his assistance and our agent 'Stan' at Jenny Brown Associates, as well as Richard Beswick and Iain Hunt at Little, Brown.

Thanks are also due to Kurt Bayer and Geraldine McKelvie of Scottish News Agency, as well as David Martin of Fotopress. Freelance Jeff Farrell did a good job in tracking down Omar Tabarez in Argentina and when I went to Argentina I was made to feel most welcome by Omar, his family and comrades. My thanks go to them all, as well as interpreters and translators Damaris Damena and Elspeth Gillespie. I would also like to thank Edgardo Esteban for his assistance and for allowing me to quote from his excellent book, *Illuminados Por El Fuego*.

ACKNOWLEDGEMENTS

I would also like to thank the good people of Liverpool who reminded me what life was all about when I visited Anfield for the *Secret Millionaire* programme. I would especially like to thank the Falkland Islanders who gave me a tremendous welcome and made me realise that it really had all been worthwhile.

My partner Maggie has encouraged me throughout and my personal assistant Cheryl Flucker has been unfailing in her assistance.

Finally, last but by no means least I would like to thank my mother and my sister Terry, along with the close friends and family who have supported me through good times and bad.

THE FORGOTTEN HIGHLANDER

Alistair Urquhart

The No.1 *Sunday Times* bestseller

Alistair Urquhart was barely twenty when he was
shipped to Singapore with the Gordon Highlanders, the
sheltered Scottish lad's war began as an exotic colonial
lifestyle of plantations, cocktails and dancehalls.

But in 1942 the Japanese invaded, and he was taken prisoner
and sent to work on the notorious Bridge over the River Kwai.
Urquhart survived starvation, cholera and the torture and brutality
of the Japanese Imperial Army, only to be packed in the hold
of a rusting hell-ship bound for Japan.

Torpedoed by an American submarine in the shark-infested
waters of the South China Sea, he drifted for days, close to death.
When he was eventually recaptured, Urquhart was transported
to a prison camp only eleven miles from a fateful city called
Nagasaki, where he bore witness to one of the most
momentous and terrible actions of human history.

ABACUS
978-0-349-12257-1

Now you can order superb titles directly from Abacus

☐ The Forgotten Highlander   Alistair Urquhart   £8.99

The price shown above is correct at time of going to press. However, the publishers reserve the right to increase prices on covers from those previously advertised, without further notice.

———————————— ⟨ABACUS⟩ ————————————

Please allow for postage and packing: **Free UK delivery.**
Europe: add 25% of retail price; Rest of World: 45% of retail price.

To order any of the above or any other Abacus titles, please call our credit card orderline or fill in this coupon and send/fax it to:

Abacus, PO Box 121, Kettering, Northants NN14 4ZQ
Fax: 01832 733076   Tel: 01832 737526
Email: aspenhouse@FSBDial.co.uk

☐ I enclose a UK bank cheque made payable to Abacus for £ . . . .
☐ Please charge £ . . . . . . to my Visa/Delta/Maestro

Expiry Date ☐☐☐☐   Maestro Issue No. ☐☐

NAME (BLOCK LETTERS please) . . . .

ADDRESS . . . .

. . . .

. . . .

Postcode . . . . Telephone . . . .

Signature . . . .

Please allow 28 days for delivery within the UK. Offer subject to price and availability.